NO ART

Also by Ben Lerner

FICTION
Leaving the Atocha Station
10:04

NON-FICTION
The Hatred of Poetry
Blossom (with Thomas Demand)

NO ART
Poems

BEN LERNER

GRANTA

Granta Publications, 12 Addison Avenue, London W11 4QR
First published in Great Britain by Granta Books 2016

Individual poems first appeared in various publications,
the details of which can be found on p.283.

A CIP catalogue record is available from the British Library

9 8 7 6 5 4 3 2 1

ISBN 978 1 78378 274 1
eISBN 978 1 78378 275 8

www.grantabooks.com

Typeset by M Rules

Printed and bound by CPI Group (UK) Ltd, Croydon, CR0 4YY

for c. d. wright

CONTENTS

INDEX OF THEMES

Poems about night
and related poems. Paintings
      about night,
sleep, death, and
           the stars.
I know one poem from
school under the stars, but
belong to no school
      of poetry.
I forgot it by heart. I remember only
it was set in the world and its theme
      parted.

      Poems
about stars and
how they are erased by street
lights,
      streets
in a poem about force
and the schools within it. We learned
all about night in college,
      how it applies,
night college under the stars where we
      made love
a subject. I completed my study of form

      and forgot it.
Tonight,
      poems about summer
and the stars are sorted by era
over me.
      Also poems about grief
and dance. I thought I'd come to you

with these themes
  like my senses.
Do you remember me
from the world?
  I was set there and we spoke

on the green, likening something
  to prison, something
to film.
  Poems about dreams
like moths about street lights
until the clichés
  glow, soft
glow of the screen
comes off on our hands,
  blue prints on the windows.
How pretentious
  to be alive now,

  let alone again
like poetry and poems
  indexed by
cadences falling about us while
parting. It was important to part
yesterday
  in a serial work about lights
so that distance could enter the voice
and address you
  tonight.
Poems about you, prose
  poems.

THE LICHTENBERG FIGURES

for Eric, Ed, Stephen, and Cy

§

The dark collects our empties, empties our ashtrays.
Did you mean "this could go on forever" in a good way?
Up in the fragrant rafters, moths seek out a finer dust.
Please feel free to cue or cut

the lights. Along the order of magnitudes, a glyph,
portable, narrow — Damn. I've lost it. But its shadow. Cast
in the long run. As the dark touches us up.
Earlier you asked if I would enter the data like a room, well,

either the sun has begun to burn
its manuscripts or I'm an idiot, an idiot
with my eleven semiprecious rings. Real snow
on the stage. Fake blood on the snow. Could this go

on forever in a good way? A brain left lace from age or lightning.
The chicken is a little dry and/or you've ruined my life.

§

I had meant to apologize in advance.
I had meant to jettison all dogmatism in theory and all sclerosis in organization.
I had meant to place my hand in a position to receive the sun.
I imagined such a gesture would amount to batter, battery. A cookie

is not the only substance that receives the shape
of the instrument with which it's cut. The man-child tucks
a flare gun into his sweatpants and sets out
for a bench of great beauty and peacefulness.

Like the girl my neighbors sent to Catholic school, tonight
the moon lies down with any boy who talks of leaving town.
My cowardice may or may not have a concrete economic foundation.
I beat Orlando Duran with a ratchet till he bled from his eye.

I like it when you cut the crust off my sandwiches.
The name of our state flower changes as it dries.

§

In my day, we knew how to drown plausibly,
to renounce the body's seven claims to buoyancy. In my day,
our fragrances had agency, our exhausted clocks complained so beautifully
that cause began to shed its calories

like sparks. With great ostentation, I began to bald. With great ostentation,
I built a small door in my door for dogs. In my day,
we were reasonable men. Even you women and children
were reasonable men. And there was the promise of pleasure in every question
we postponed. Like a blouse, the most elegant crimes were left undone.

Now I am the only one who knows
the story of the baleful forms
our valences assumed in winter light. My people, are you not

horrified of how these verbs decline—
their great ostentation, their doors of different sizes?

§

What am I the antecedent of?
When I shave I feel like a Russian.
When I drink I'm the last Jew in Kansas.
I sit in my hammock and whittle my rebus.
I feel disease spread through me like a theory.
I take a sip from Death's black daiquiri.

Darling, my favorite natural abstraction is a tree
so every time you see one from the highway
remember the ablative case in which I keep
your tilde. (A scythe of moon divides
the cloud. The story regains its upward sweep.)
O slender spadix projecting from a narrow spathe,

you are thinner than spaghetti but not as thin as vermicelli.
You are the first and last indigenous Nintendo.

§

We must retract our offerings, burnt as they are.
We must recall our lines of verse like faulty tires.
We must flay the curatoriat, invest our sackcloth,

and enter the Academy single file.

Poetry has yet to emerge.
The image is no substitute. The image is an anecdote
in the mouth of a stillborn. And not reflection,
with its bad infinitude, nor religion, with its eighth of mushrooms,
can bring orgasm to orgasm like poetry. As a policy,

we are generally sorry. But sorry doesn't cut it.
We must ask you to remove your shoes, your lenses, your teeth.
We must ask you to sob openly.

If it is any consolation, we admire the early work of John Ashbery.
If it is any consolation, you won't feel a thing.

§

I attend a class for mouth-to-mouth, a class for hand-to-hand.
I can no longer distinguish between combat and resuscitation.
I could revive my victims. I could kill a man
with a maneuver designed to clear the throat of food. Tonight, the moon

sulks at apogee. A bitch complains to the polestar. An enemy
fills a Ping-Pong ball with Drano and drops it in the gas tank of my car.

Reader, may your death strictly adhere to recognized forms.
May someone place his lips on yours, shake you gently, call your name.
May someone interlace his fingers, lock his elbows, and compress your chest,
every two seconds, to the depth of one and one-half inches. In the dream,

I discover my body among the abandoned tracks of North Topeka.
Orlando Duran stands over me, bleeding from his eye. I can no longer
        distinguish

between verb moods that indicate confidence and those that express uncertainty.
An upward emergency calls away the sky.

§

Pleasure is a profoundly negative experience, my father
was fond of saying underwater. His body was carried out
like a wish. We paid our last respects
as rent. The mere possibility of apology allows me to express
my favorite wreck as a relation between stairs
and stars. I take that back. To sum up, up

beyond the lamp's sweep, where a drip installed by heat
still drips—some tender timbers. At thirteen, I had a series
of dreams I can't remember, although I'm sure
that they involved a rape. I'm brutal because I'm naked,
not because I'm named, a distinction
that the scientific and scholarly communities,
if not the wider public, should be expected to maintain.
No additional media available (but isn't it beautiful when a toddler manages to
     find and strike a match).

§

I invite you to think creatively about politics in the age of histamine.
I invite you to think creatively about politics

given men as they are: asthmatic, out of tune and time,
out of bounds and practice. I invite you to run your mouth, to run your hands
through my thin hair like a theme. I invite you to lean your head

against my better judgment. Once uncertainty
ran through these sketches like a Lab. Now, of my early work, a critic has said:

"It was open, so I let myself in." Ladies and gentlemen,

tonight's weather has been canceled. The Academy has condemned
the blue tit. The poor are stealing the saltlicks. Grenades luxuriate
in the garden of decommissioned adjectives. It is the Sabbath. I must invite you

to lay down your knowledge claims,
to lay them down slowly and with great sadness.

Given men as they are, women pack snow into jars for the summer ahead.
Given men as they are, the trees surrender.

I'm going to kill the president.
I promise. I surrender. I'm sorry.
I'm gay. I'm pregnant. I'm dying.
I'm not your father. You're fired.
Fire. I forgot your birthday.
You will have to lose the leg.
She was asking for it.
It ran right under the car.
It looked like a gun. It's contagious.
She's with God now.
Help me. I don't have a problem.
I've swallowed a bottle of aspirin.
I'm a doctor. I'm leaving you.
I love you. Fuck you. I'll change.

§

True, a great work takes up the question of its origins
and lets it drop. But this is no great work. This is a sketch
sold on the strength of its signature, a sketch
executed without a trial. Inappropriately formal,

this late work reflects an inability to swallow. Once
my name suggested female bathers
rendered in bright impasto.
Now it is dismissed as "unpronounceable."

Polemical, depressed, these contiguous black planes
were hung to disperse museum crowds. Alas,
a generation of pilgrim smokers
has arrived and set off the sprinklers.

True, abandoning the figure won't change the world.
But then again, neither will changing the world.

§

for Ronald Johnson

The sun spalls the sluiceway into shards.
The blind man finds an equivalent for adult films.
The rabbi downs a hin of wine and gives

it a rest. A votive candle is delicately set
into a small, decorative paper bag
weighted with sand and placed in a row
along the dock. The poet will never walk
again. Not even in poems.
Lightning bugs set down their loads.

Tonight the women have the feel of men
who've worked. For you I have retired a word.
It is the only word that never appeared in your books.
It was the only word you didn't know.
It begins with the letter *O*.

§

To forestall a suicide, I plant all manner
of night-blooming genera. I compose this preemptive elegy.
I describe the sky as "noctilucent." In this very elegy,
the sky is thus described.

To prevent slow singing, I rub the body down
with acacia. I pledge to hide
the man who struck the body. I threaten to use
the same rope or opiate but minutes after.

To keep the neighbors from delivering all manner
of sympathy casserole, I water the Scotch.
I hide the Drano. I no longer park
in the garage.

I discover the body prone, check its breathing.
Go back to sleep.

§

I confused her shadow for an accent.
I confused her body for a simplified prose version of *Paradise Lost.*
I confused her heritage for a false-bottom box.
I confused her weeping for express written consent. "Choked with leaves"

is the kind of thing a child would say in this rhomboid fun park and yet
you've been saying it under your breath, way under, ever since
the posse of stars rolled in. Obese with echo, Milton tips his brim.

Twenty-one years of destroying all evidence of use has produced extensive
        evidence of wear.
So I hike up my graphite trousers and set out
for an epicenter of great beauty and peacefulness. "A major event."
She called the publication of a portable version "a major event."
She called my adjusting the clasp "a major event."

She confused my powerful smell for a cry from the street.
She confused exhalation for better living through chemistry.

§

I must drive many miles to deliver this punch line.
I must drive many miles in the modern manner,

which is suicide, beneath this corrigendum of a sky. Tonight
Orlando Duran went crazy. He smeared every doorknob,
lock, and mirror in his apartment with spermicidal jelly.

To expel air from the lungs suddenly

is not to live beautifully in the modern manner. Rather
one must learn to drive, to drive
in the widest sense of the word, a sense that seats four
other senses comfortably. Tonight Orlando Duran

delivered himself in the modern manner,
delivered himself like a punch line. Is this what he meant by

"negative liberty,"
by "the sound of one hand clapping is a heartbeat"?

§

Possessing a weapon has made me bashful.

Tears appreciate in this economy of pleasure.

The ether of data engulfs the capitol.

Possessing a weapon has made me forgetful.

My oboe tars her cenotaph.

The surface is in process.

Coruscant skinks emerge in force.

The moon spits on a copse of spruce.

Plausible opposites stir in the brush.

Jupiter spins in its ruts.

The wind extends its every courtesy.

I have never been here.

Understand?

You have never seen me.

§

The sky is a big responsibility. And I am the lone intern. This explains
my drinking. This explains my luminous portage, my baboon heart
that breaks nightly like the news. Who

am I kidding? I am Diego Rodríguez Velázquez. I am a dry
and eviscerated analysis of the Russian Revolution.
I am line seven. And my memory, like a melon,
contains many dark seeds. Already, this poem has achieved

the status of lore amongst you little people of New England. Nevertheless,
I, Dr. Samuel Johnson, experience moments of such profound alienation
that I have surrendered my pistols to the care of my sister, Elisabeth Förster-
    Nietzsche.

Forgive me. For I have taken things too far. And now your carpet is ruined.
Forgive me. For I am not who you think I am. I am Charlie Chaplin

playing a waiter embarrassed by his occupation. And when the rich woman I
    love
enters this bistro, I must pretend that I'm only pretending to play a waiter for
    her amusement.

§

The abolition of perspective is an innovation in perspective.
Found matter invades the middle distance.
Yet long after perspective has rigidified
perspective is propped up and televised. As if the painter
were an epiphenomenon of gesture. For many years,

we lacked an adequate theory of decline
and affected spiritual gloom
with a turbulent cross-layering of brushwork.
Then, with the invention of the camera, we began to cry.

Here a woman emerges from the surface plane, invites our gaze,
and disappears. Here a woman succumbs
to her own frenetic coloration. The pictorial attack

on closed systems is a closed system.
Found matter invades the middle distance.

§

When a longing exceeds its object, a suburb is founded.
Goatsuckers spar in the linden. The redskins are hunted.
When the hunt exceeds its object, the past achieves
pubescence. History pauses
for emphasis. After these poems are published,

money will be no object.
Money will be a gray bird known for mocking other birds.
The stars will be adjusted for inflation
so that the dead can continue living
in the manner to which they've grown accustomed.

When a dream of convenience begins to dream itself,
the neighborhood's last bamboos reel in their roots.
The children make love "execution style,"
then hold each other like moments of silence.

§

Your child lacks a credible god-term, a jargon of ultimacy.
He fails to distinguish between illusion (*Schein*) and beautiful illusion (*schöner
Schein*).
He is inept and unattractive.
Today I asked your child to depress

the right pedal, to stop the action of the dampers
so that the strings could vibrate freely. In response he struck me
in the stomach with a pipe.

Your child is a bereavement arbitrarily prescribed,
a hyperkinetic disorder expressed in chromatic variations.
By the age of twenty-three, your child will be bald
and dead. He's a bright boy and eager to learn. But bourgeois spectator forms

have supplanted the music of the salon,
inciting a sheer vertical sonority
that has dispatched the theme to keys beyond his reach.

§

Resembling a mobile but having no mobile parts,
my instrument for measuring potential differences (in volts)
is like a songbird in a Persian poem. I have absolutely no

idea what I'm saying. I know only
that I have a certain sympathy
for the rhetoric of risk and mystery. Think of my body

as a local institution. Think of my body
as a monocoque. Think of my body
as the ponderous surgeons of Wichita

ready their nibs. When the first starlings began to cough up blood,
the night applied its cataplasm. The moon issued its scrip
to the Austrian dead. An expert described your son

as incapable of some really important shit.
Your son described his name in the air with a spliff.

§

They can take your life, but not your life signs, my father
was fond of saying after apnea. But that was before articles
shifted during flight, before our graphs
grew indistinguishable from our appetites. In fine,
that was the greatest period of American prosperity

since my depression. Father's left hand was an extension
of liberal thinking. It could strike a man without assuming
a position on the good. His left hand was a complete
and austere institution. In fine, it could move through

my body's DMZs without detection. But that was before
articles copped pleas and feels from objects, objects
rendered fulgent by our theories, back before my mood

swung slowly open
to let this ether enter like a view.

§

The poetic establishment has co-opted contradiction.
And the poetic establishment has not co-opted contradiction.
Are these poems just cumbersome
or are these poems a critique of cumbersomeness?

The sky stops painting and turns to criticism.
We envy the sky its contradictions. We envy the sky
its exposed patches of unprimed canvas
and their implicit critique of painterly finish.

It is raining for emphasis. Or it is raining emphases
on a public ill-prepared for the cubist accomplishment.
Perhaps what remains of innovation
is a conservatism at peace with contradiction,

as the sky transgresses its frame
but obeys the museum.

§

"Gather your marginals, Mr. Specific. The end
is nigh. Your vanguard of vanishing points has vanished
in the critical night. We have encountered a theory
of plumage with plumage. We have decentered our ties. You must quit
these Spenglerian Suites, this roomy room, this gloomy Why.
Never again will your elephants shit in the embassy.
Never again will you cruise through Topeka in your sporty two-door coffin.
In memoriam, we will leave the laws you've broken broken."

On vision and modernity in the twentieth century, my mother wrote
"Help me." On the history of structuralism my father wrote
"Settle down." On the American Midwest from 1979 to the present, I wrote
"Gather your marginals, Mr. Specific. The end is nigh."

I wish all difficult poems were profound.
Honk if you wish all difficult poems were profound.

§

for Benjamin

Sensation dissolves into sense through this idle discussion,
into a sense that sees itself and is afraid. Still, we must finish our coffee
and partition epiphany
into its formative mistakes. Reclining on my detention-camp pallet,

I dream in Hebrew of a cigarette
that restores immediacy to the theoretical domain.
Or, if that strikes you as immodest, I purchase a portable classic
and interpret it loosely
until the infinite takes place. Recent criticism understates

the importance of our coffee,
how it removes transcendence from beneath our pillows
and leaves us a pointless enigma or silver dollar in its stead.

The stars are a mnemonic without object.
Let the forgetting begin.

§

for Benjamin

The forgetting begins.
Infinitives are hewn from events.
The letters of your name fall asleep at their posts.
The dead vote in new members. Police declaw your books.

A suspicious white powder is mailed to the past,
forcing its closure. In order to avoid exposure,
I use the present tense. Sense grows sentimental
at the prospect of deferral. The stars dehisce.

By "stars" I mean, of course, *tradition,*
and by "tradition" I mean nothing at all.
A pronoun disembowels his antecedent.
Stop me if you've heard this one before.

Your body is broken by exegesis.
The thinkable goes sobbing door-to-door.

§

for Benjamin

The thinkable goes sobbing door-to-door
in search of predicates accessible by foot.
But sense is much shorter in person
and retreats from chamber to antechamber to text.

How then to structure a premise like a promise?

The heroic negativity of pleasure
is that it makes my body painfully apparent,
a body that weighs six hundred pounds on Jupiter
and next to nothing here in Europe.

How then to justify our margins?

Some cultures use quotation marks for warmth.
In ours they've withered without falling off.
The trees apologize each autumn,
but nature can never be sorry enough.

§

What, if not the derivative, will keep us warm? The tragic interchangeability of
    nouns?
The breastbone? Two vanguards sharing a bathroom?

When I first found the subjunctive, she was broke and butt-naked.
Now she wants half. She wants her own set of keys
and bullets designed to expand on impact.

A pamphlet of sparks? The National Book Award?

Meaning is a child of my third marriage. A marriage of convenience.
A wartime marriage. We had plastic champagne flutes and no champagne.
A staple instead of a ring. A dialectician in place of a priest.

A butter substitute? Rogaine for women?

Consider the rain my resignation. I regret having founded Cubism.
I regret the lines I broke by the eye
and the lines I broke by the breath.

The hair around the vulva? Proust in translation? September 11th?

§

Announcing a late style as distinctive as the late style of Matisse,
my grandfather no longer speaks.
The figure in my grandfather's memory has disappeared completely.
It has been replaced with a kind of allover abstraction
made up of broad and colorful strokes. Critics agree

that my grandfather's exaggerated midsection and useless legs
constitute a critique of consumer society,
that his body's adoption of chance procedures
signals a rejection of his former realist sympathies.

"The progressive surrender of the resistance of the medium
and the exclusion of all techniques extraneous to the medium"
is one way to conceive of artistic modernity:
critics identify the essence of painting with flatness;
sculpture, they argue, rests in peace.

Now to defend a bit of structure: beeline, skyline, dateline, saline—
now to torch your effluent shanty
so the small rain down can rain. I'm so Eastern that my Ph.D.
has edible tubers, my heart a hibachi oiled with rapeseed. I'm so Western that
    my Ph.D.

can bang and bank all ball game, bringing the crowd to its feet
and the critics to their knees. Politically speaking, I'm kind of an animal.
I feed the ducks duck meat in duck sauce when I walk to clown school in my
    clown shoes.
The Germans call me Ludwig, bearer of estrus, the northern kingdom's
professional apologist. The Germans call me Benji, the radical browser,
alcoholic groundskeeper of the Providence Little League. All readers of poetry

are Germans, are virgins. All readers of poetry sicken me. You, with your Soviet
    Ph.D.
and Afghan tiepin. You with your penis stuck in a bottle. And yes, of course, I
    sicken me,
with my endless and obvious examples
of the profound cultural mediocrity of the American bourgeoisie.

§

Beauty cannot account for how the sparkplug works.
But if the sparkplug doesn't work, it is more beautiful.
If I display a sparkplug, it is sculpture.
A sparkplug sculpture may be a real sparkplug,
but the sculpture refers to other sculptures, while the sparkplug refers
to an engine cylinder.
The word "sparkplug" is an altogether different matter.

Thus I return to the subject of the museum.
A woman is crying in the Surrealist wing.
Beauty cannot account for why the woman is crying.
But because the woman is crying, she is more beautiful.
Is the woman therefore a work of Surrealist sculpture?
A sculpture of a woman may be a real woman,
but the sculpture refers to other sculptures, while the woman refers

§

You say "ablution," I say "ablation."
You say "gloaming," I say "crepuscule."
You say "organ of copulation," I say "organ of excretion."
You say "forget-me-not," I say "scorpion grass."
While you were at tennis camp, I was finger-banged

by a six-fingered man. I replaced your dead goldfish
with another dead goldfish. I put your dad in a headlock
and your mom in a home. I ate your juicy motherfucking plums.

Irreconcilable differences: you disliked the Richter show.
Your gait is characterized by an exaggerated flexion of the knee.

I really don't want to do this over the phone.
But I also never want to see you again.
So I paid Ben Lerner to write you this poem
in language that was easy to understand.

§

To attend carefully to Celan in the airport terminal.
To admire the aspen in the atrium. This adjective
for that anguish. The unnatural attitudes
of the sleeping tourist. Remember

the '80s? We hit rewind
and the snow refused the ground.
We were all of us speaking German,
we were all of us wearing licensed sport apparel.

Some took your absence in stride. Some took it
lying down. Some took it with milk
and sugar. Only your wife took it like a man.

My flight originated in Denver.
My flight is now boarding. My flight is now slowly
pushing away from the gate.

§

To assimilate sculpture to sepulture, sublimity to sublation,
to ululate sub judice, to inurn in utero,
as if the absence of birds in the poem were the absence of birds in the world,
as if et cetera were an aesthetics. Ad interim,
shadows cast shadows ad infinitum. Ad absurdum,

eye-contact counts as coitus, neologism as parturition.
To squander the mind's ultimate candela on the mimetic.
To simply hurl paint at the canvas
as if it were a blackbody absorbing incident radiants,
as if in vino veritas quod erat demonstrandum nonsense as death wish,
nonsense as warm-blooded egg-laying winged and feathered vertebrate.

Now with handicap access to the principal texts,
principal texts posthumously signed.
Now with expanded signature in bilingual remission.

§

The left hand is a scandal. And my woman is left-handed.
She neglects our middle children.
She deploys her powers on behalf of other nations.
Sleep is a synagogue. And my woman sleeps
the dreamless sleep of the pornographer. Mother always said,

"Worship me, and all this will be yours." Father always said,
"Suffer common hardship and die in bed."
Yet I reside with my woman on her acre of irony.
Yet I will die on the cross and I worship my death.

The Internet is the future. And my woman rejects the Internet.
She rises up when I lie down.
She inflames divisions among the Jews.
Citation is exaltation. And my woman cites
her own unpublished dissertation.

§

I posit the notion of progress so I can experience decline.
I sport my underwear on the outside of my trousers.
My hybrid form has become a genre in its own right.
I squander my disposable income on redundant social services.
After the dissolution of feudal society, moonlight emerges

as the symbolic locus of heroic individualism.
I transform absurd contingency into historical necessity with box wine.
My facility with parataxis makes me respected, feared.
I send my professor thirty dollars' worth of fusiform compound umbels
after her only child is shot and killed. Interwar experiments with collage

reflect increasing disenchantment with the sensible world.
A wasp attacks me using her ovipositor as a sting.
I strike a teenager with a baseball bat to gain blue-collar credibility.
I feel dirty reading on the toilet.

§

I place a terminal raceme of fragrant, funnel-shaped perianths
beside the mile marker where Orlando flipped his Honda.
I fuck his girlfriend and induce epistaxis in his homeboy.

You asked me to explain the peculiar power of continental literary criticism,
to clarify what I mean by "theory" in the sentence
"To clarify what I mean by *theory* in the sentence."

The impossibility of referring to the interruption immanent in the referential
        chain.
Snowfall in North Topeka.
The impossibility of not referring to the immanent interruption.
Real persons, living or dead, resembled coincidentally.

Orlando imbued my body with erotic significance
by beating it with a pistol. Nothing is as metaphysical
as the claim to break from metaphysics. At a party in his honor,
we throw our hands in the air. We wave them like we just don't care.

§

Then bullets tore through the soft tissue of our episteme.
We had thought that by arranging words at random
we could avoid ideology. We were right.
Then we were terribly wrong. Such is the nature of California.

What I remember most about the Renaissance
is that everything had tits. Streetcars, sunsets,
everything. Defacing a medium
just for the F of it—
that was my idea. It was 1865;
no one was worried about positivism.

You can argue with our methods
but not with our methodology.
So a couple of janitors lost their legs.
Today, some of my best friends are janitors.

§

"Is this seat taken?" I don't understand the question.

"Was there ever any doubt?" Below the knees.

"Can you forgive me?" I hardly even know you.

"Does it have meat in it?" I'm not at liberty to say.

"Am I going to be OK?" Yes and no.

"How long was I asleep?" That remains to be seen.

"Have you met my mother?" I won't dignify that with an answer.

"Do you love me?"

"Which would you prefer?" Long ago.

"Can you hear me?" In the pejorative sense.

"How do I know it's really you?" Not exactly.

"Did you do the reading?" I do not love you.

"Swear on your life?" Swear on my life.

"Do you want me to leave?" Little by little.

§

King of Beers, King of Pop, King of Kings;
proud sponsor of rain dance and mercy killing,
Special Olympiad and circumcision;
moviegoer, meat eater, Republican: bless

my girlfriend, bless each chicken finger, the commute
to Brooklyn, watch over her hard drive and suspicious mole,
forgive her smoking, protect her from anthrax
and obesity, Scud and Rohypnol. If she is groped at a bar,
if she is cursed by a cabbie, if she loses her job,

repeal the moon, send a plague through nicotine patch
and cell phone, empty your seven bowls on the G7,
numb the penis, crash an airliner into the North Star. Destroy
with fire, short sword, and sulfur, then destroy
fire, short sword, and sulfur. Destroy me. Then destroy her.

§

In those days partial nudity was permitted
provided the breasts in question hung from indigenes.

The clouds had an ease of diction,
and Death had a way with women,
and at night our documents opened
to emit their redolent confessions.

In those days whole onions, whole peoples were immersed
in the pellucid, semisolid fat of hogs.

The children ran lines of powdered gold,
huffed glue composed of studs,
smoked burial myrrh, and then shot up
their schools.

In those days police hauled in all bugs, then birds, then stars,
and the sky fled underground.

§

Idle elevators of grain. Plenty of parking. Deciduous trees
of the genus *Ulmus,* known for their arching branches and serrate leaves
with asymmetrical bases. Gunplay in our houses of steak,
houses of pancakes. Dried valerian rhizomes. Bunk weed. Osage.

Deliberately elliptical poetic works reflect a fear of political commitment after
        1968.
A fear of deliberately elliptical poetic works reflects...

Home considered as a system of substitutions: "Plenty of parking.
Deciduous elevators of the genus *Gunplay,*
known for their arching bases and serrate pancakes
with asymmetrical rhizomes." The activation of the white space of the page

reflects a fear of the industrialization of print media.
To fear the activation of the white space of the page

is to fear poetry.
Idle elliptical commitment. Deciduous repetition. Plenty of parking.

§

Blood on the time that we have on our hands.
Blood on our sheets, our sheets of music.
Blood on the canvases
of boxing rings, the canvases of Henri Matisse.

The man-child faints at the sight of blood
and so must close his eyes
as he dispatches his terrier
with a pocketknife. Tonight,

blood condensed from atmospheric vapor
falls to the earth. It bleeds three inches.
Concerts are canceled, ball games delayed.
In galoshes and slickers, the children play.

An arc of seven spectral colors appears opposite the sun
as a result of light refracted through the drops of blood.

§

The author gratefully acknowledges the object world.
Acknowledgment is gratefully made
to *Sleep: A Journal of Sleep.*
The author wishes to thank the foundation,
which poured its money into the sky.
A grant from the sky made this project impossible.

Lerner, Benjamin, 1979–1945
  The Lichtenberg figures / Benjamin Lerner.
      p. cm.
  ISBN 1-55659-211-6 (pbk. : alk. paper)
  I. Title.
  PS2343.E23432A6 1962
  911'.01–dc43   52-28544
  CIP

§

My death was first runner-up at the 1996 Kansas State Wrestling Championships
     (157 lbs).
My death is the author of *César Vallejo: The Complete Posthumous Poetry.*
My death was the first death in my family
to ever graduate from college.
My death graduated from the University of California, Berkeley.

Your death was the 1996 Kansas State Wrestling Champion (157 lbs).
Your death is the author of César Vallejo's *Trilce.*
Your death was the third death in your family
to deliver a commencement address
at the University of California, Berkeley.

Her death doesn't care about your death's fame or physique.
Her death is the author of *Tungsten,* César Vallejo's social-realist experiment.
Her death likes to run her hands through what's left of my death's hair.
Her death would like to start a family.

§

She left town. Rain ensued. Crows pecked out my contacts.
I tried everything: Prozac, plainsong. I won her back.
It didn't help. I shot myself. It didn't help.
A beauty incommensurate with syntax
had whupped my cracker ass.

When I was fair and young and favor graced me
my fingers were in everybody's mouth.
Ten fat fingers in ten fat mouths.
Now my fingers just point stuff out.

She shot herself. And, with a typically raucous cry,
her glossy, black body fell from the typical sky.
It fell like rain. It was rain. Fat drops of rain rained down
into my fat awaiting mouth.
It didn't help.

§

In my culture, when a woman dies, we sleep on the floor.
We sleep with her sister. We put her cats to sleep.
We tear at our hair. We tear at the hair of others.
We pass roseate urinary calculi. We dream ourselves hoarse.

In my culture, when a woman dies,
we mash the effervescent abdomens of fireflies
into mascara for the long-lashed corpse.

Virga is customary. Light opera is customary.
An exchange of fluids, of fire, is customary. It is customary to spike
the Berry Blue Kool-Aid with cyanide. Customarily,
starlings collide. And yes, of course,

after the potluck, when we've put the children to sleep,
we bathe the widower in lilac, dress him in bombazine,
and reduce him to ash.

§

The light lines up to die. The light dies down.
Out of embarrassment, the light dies out.
At 7:32 CST, the light is pronounced dead.
The light's death is pronounced

"Ayúdame."

The first female president was César Vallejo.
César Vallejo was the first African American in space.
Indicted child pornographer, César Vallejo.
Vallejo, aka Eshleman, aka Lerner.

Perdóname.

The endless miserable progression of Thursdays.
Miserable progression of glottal stops.
That "palindrome" is not a palindrome.
Endless miserable progression of decimals.

§

In the early '00s, my concern with abstraction
culminated in a series of public exhalations.
I was praised for my use of repetition. But, alas,
my work was understood.

Then the towers collapsed
and antimissile missiles tracked
the night sky with ellipses.

I decided that what we needed was a plain style,
not more condoms stuffed with chocolate frosting.
After six months in my studio, I emerged
and performed a series of public exhalations.

Only time will tell
if my work is representational.
Only time will tell if time will tell.

§

It is always already winter.
Raccoons open each other for warmth.
The poor live under the bridge outside of time.
If we can speak of the poor. If you can call that a bridge.
At a fashionable retrospective, a woman soils her prewar dress.

In order to avoid saying "I," the author eats incessantly.
The author experiences pleasure from a great distance,
like the bombing of an embassy. In the business district,
fire is exchanged. The media butcher the suspect's name.

Every weekend, the law gets laid,
while these abstractions, hung like horses,
attend their semiformals stag. The last census

counts several selves inhabiting this gaze,
mostly unemployed.

§

Forgotten in advance, these failures are technological
in the oldest sense: they allow us to see ourselves as changed
and to remain unchanged. These failures grant us

an unwelcome reprieve
and now we must celebrate wildly
until we are bereft.

As in, "Beauty rears her ugly head."
As in, "I broke her arm so I could sign the cast."

There is suffering somewhere else,
but here in Kansas our acquaintances
rape us tenderly and remain unchanged.

Will these failures grow precious through repetition
and, although we cannot hope to be forgiven,
will these failures grow precious through repetition?

§

I did it for the children. I did it for the money.
I did it for the depression of spirit and the cessation of hope.
I did it because I could, because it was there.
I'd do it again. Oops, I did it again.

What have I done? What have I done
to deserve this? What have I done with my keys,
my youth? What am I going to do
while you're at tennis camp? What are we going to do

with the body? I don't do smack. I don't do
toilets. I don't do well at school. I could do
with a bath. Unto others, I do
injurious, praiseworthy, parroted acts.

Let's just do Chinese. Just do as I say. Just do me.
That does it. Easy does it. That'll do.

§

The sky narrates snow. I narrate my name in the snow.
Snow piled in paragraphs. Darkling snow. Geno-snow
and pheno-snow. I staple snow to the ground.

In medieval angelology, there are nine orders of snow.
A vindication of snow in the form of snow.
A jealous snow. An omni-snow. Snow immolation.

Do you remember that winter it snowed?
There were bodies everywhere. Obese, carrot-nosed.
A snow of translucent hexagonal signifiers. Meta-snow.

Sand replaced with snow. Snowpaper. A window of snow
opened onto the snow. Snow replaced with sand.
A sandman. Obese, carrot-nosed. Tiny swastikas

of snow. Vallejo's unpublished snow.
Real snow on the stage. Fake blood on the snow.

ANGLE OF YAW

for my parents

for my brother

in memory of Rose

Printing, having found in the book a refuge in which to lead an autonomous existence, is pitilessly dragged out onto the street... If centuries ago it began gradually to lie down, passing from the upright inscription to the manuscript resting on sloping desks before finally taking to bed in the printed book, it now begins just as slowly to rise again from the ground. The newspaper is read more in the vertical than in the horizontal plane, while film and advertisement force the printed word entirely into the dictatorial perpendicular.

Walter Benjamin, "One-way Street"

Frosted eyes there were that lifted altars;
And silent answers crept across the stars.

Hart Crane, "At Melville's Tomb"

I

BEGETTING STADIA

for Marjorie Welish

Demands indefinitely specified,
demands incompatible with collective living

beget stadia
with indefinite seating
delicately tiered.

Resembling its shape
and therefore suggesting its function:

a wave.

Or repeating its shape
and therefore undoing its function:

a wave,

which I will here attempt to situate
in the broader cognitive process
of turning the page.

Just because these tears were on your face
doesn't mean they're yours.
The tree in your mind

is mine.
The redistribution of tears
reflects our collective commitment

to storm and stress,
to attitudes befitting participants in sports

and sports writing.
The conventions governing weeping in novels
do not apply to weeping done on-camera

or in teams.
Eldest sons dispossessed of ancestral tears
mock the tears of the nouveaux riches.
You call that weeping?

We call it sports entertainment
because the loser gets paid more,
because losing is hazardous,
because hazards are for losers

in the collective economy
of variable stars.

Rational actors wearing wrestling masks
would choose to lose collectively,
to collectivize losing
in the service industry.

I perform a valuable service
(I lose)
and I work from home.

Am I not then entitled to drink six beers
and watch some losing gracefully performed?

The sorcerer's apprentice is an animated mouse
losing control over water-toting brooms.
Now, what does that say about cleaning?

Sorcery cuts grease and glass like lightning!

Now, who will clean up this water?
What will we use to remove this water
from our jerseys? I suggest sorcery.

My Little League team is made up of animated mice
losing control of their jerseys
and delaying the game with lightning
in the manner of Fabius and Disney.

General Disney gets clothes clean (with sorcery).
General Disney's Chicken (with sorcery sauce).

The novel hurled to the ground breaks into verse
and achieves a perfect synthesis

of Bible and phonebook,
a chance synthesis
recalling the work of X
in its use of cherry and adverb.

A branch of adverb negatively rendered
is characteristic of a period
in which phonebooks possess all the qualities of epics

plus or minus three.
X is of that generation that gloried in synthesis
privately performed,
in charity syntheses held for cherry trees.

I have chopped down the truth conditions for cherry trees
with a chance synthesis,

with a phonebook in one hand
and a Bible in the other
and the other.

Configured to return to the thrower when hurled
and configured to return the thrower to the herd,

intended backfires configure warmth
for the polis and polis fans.
Context attributed to the skin at birth

picks teams:
shirts and skins,
redshirts and redskins
and tomahawking redskin fans.

"In 1825, the natives of Port Jackson hurled their halos and lay down."
Support your polis: chop the air.

The roof fell in
medias res.

We fled
into the trees.

But that part of
roof that was ceiling

that was glass,
we carry with us

here, he said,
touching his head

to his heart.
The roof fell in

in place and we
fled *here*

and *here,*
carrying our heads

in our hands,
holding our hands

to the light,
to that part of light

that was glass
and fell in

absentia.

II

ANGLE OF YAW

THE PREDICTABILITY OF THESE ROOMS is, in a word, exquisite. These rooms in a word. The moon is predictably exquisite, as is the view of the moon through the word. Nevertheless, we were hoping for less. Less space, less light. We were hoping to pay more, to be made to pay in public. We desire a flat, affected tone. A beware of dog on keep off grass. The glass ceiling is exquisite. Is it made of glass? No, glass.

THE BIRD'S-EYE VIEW abstracted from the bird. Cover me, says the soldier on the screen, I'm going in. We have the sense of being convinced, but of what? And by whom? The public is a hypothetical hole, a realm of pure disappearance, from which celestial matter explodes. I believe I can speak for everyone, begins the president, when I say famous last words.

ALL ACROSS AMERICA, from under- and aboveground, from burning buildings and deep wells, hijacked planes and collapsed mines, people are using their cell phones to call out, not for help or air or light, but for information.

IN THE EARLIEST FILMS, ACTORS PRETEND to accomplish prodigious acrobatic feats by rolling around on a black carpet while being filmed from above. The prophet who seems to ascend to heaven is being dragged across the floor. The first generation of moviegoers was unable to decipher the action on the screen, despite the *explicador*. The second generation mistook them for real grapes. In order to reproduce the colors of nature in our films, we have painted nature black and white. Startle the cuttlefish. Harvest the sepia. The literal color of fear.

ALL WE REMEMBER OF OUR CHILDHOOD is sliding down inclined chutes mounted by means of ladders, down slick chutes terminating in pools of water, across wet tarps laid atop the lawn, across hardwood floors in our socks, on short boards equipped with wheels, on roller skates, on ice skates, on ice, on gravel.

THE FIRST GAMING SYSTEM was the domesticated flame. Contemporary video games allow you to select the angle from which you view the action, inspiring a rash of high school massacres. Newer games, with their use of small strokes to simulate reflected light, are all but unintelligible to older players. We have abstracted airplanes from our simulators in the hope of manipulating flight as such. Game cheats, special codes that make your character invincible or rich, alter weather conditions or allow you to bypass a narrative stage, stand in relation to video games as prayer to reality. Children, if pushed, will attempt to inflict game cheats on the phenomenal world. Enter up, down, up, down, left, right, left, right, a, b, a, to tear open the sky. Left, left, b, b, to keep warm.

SHE WILL NEVER WANT FOR MONEY. Her uncle invented the room. On our first date, I told the one about the dead astronaut. How was I supposed to know? To prepare the air for her image, I put on soft music. I use gum to get the gum out of my hair. Like every exfoliated smear, we must either be stained or invisible. Maybe we should see other people? Impossible. The new trains don't touch their tracks. The new razors don't touch the cheek. If I want to want you, isn't that enough? No. Way too much.

HE HAD ENOUGH RESPECT FOR PAINTING to quit. Enough respect for quitting to paint. Enough respect for the figure to abstract. For abstraction to hint at the breast. For the breast to ask the model to leave. But I live here, says the model. And I respect that, says the painter. But I have enough respect for respect to insist. For insistence to turn the other cheek. For the other cheek to turn the other cheek. Hence I appear to be shaking my head *No.*

MINUTE PARTICLES OF DEBRIS IN SLOW DESCENT force evacuation of the concept. At what altitude does the view grow comprehensive? The daredevil places his head in the camera, eliciting oohs and aahs. We have willingly suspended our disbelief on strings in order to manipulate it from above.

IT IS WITH SOME DIFFIDENCE the author offers his public to the work. The tree remains where it was felled: inside the head, standing. For if my race provides an extensive field for theory, our rhymes are no less trash. The author retains no ill will toward the Gypsy people, nor a will in general. Without enthusiasm, we have chosen enthusiasm over truth. After dinner, straight to winter. Sidi Habismilk, I have searched the Internet. Nothing indicates your God is sorry. That's because our God is sorrow. In one palm, a lake of fire. In the other, a posthumous issue.

THE MASSIVE SWASTIKA, twenty meters in size, can only be seen from the air in autumn, when the larch trees turn a yellowish brown and stand out against the evergreen forest. Had the pattern been sown in the distant past, it would have been visible only to a higher being. At halftime, the marching band assumes a formation fully legible only to the blimp. But the blimp communicates the image of the field to a giant screen, allowing the crowd to perceive the flag formed by the musicians. The displacement of the horizontal plane by the vertical plane: the displacement of the God-term by the masses.

DEAR CYRUS, HE PUTS DOWN, DEAR CYRUS, yesterday while taking the, he puts down, air in the company of M. de Charlus, your cousin, the Baron, that is, while taking a spin, he puts down, in the motorcar, which respects no mystery, to Thun, he puts down, to the town of T, and the children trailing the, he puts down, which respects no, and the children playing with smoke on a string, frozen smoke on a stick, your cousin the Baron, drew my attention, my attention, you understand, was drawn, there was a silver, and the children screaming, flying machine, in terror, he puts down, with pleasure, and in the eyes of the cousin, your Baron, who respects no, who is no, displayed like, longer, objects, tears, of price, remain your, humble servant, I

THE PORTION OF THE STORY THAT REMAINS after the other components have been dissolved by churning. The woman attends the night game to watch the snow fall near the lights. Only the body of the protagonist is undergoing change. A whistle sweeps the town of meaning.

THE AVERAGE READER only perceives the initial and final letters of a word. He only reads the longest and most peculiar words in a sentence, intuiting the remaining language. The average reader often turns two pages at once, without perceiving a breach in narrative. He picks up a book, quickly flips through its pages, and believes it read. Conversely, he often reads unawares, will process and even vocalize a text he believes himself to be composing, while in fact reading skywriting, between the lines, on the wall. In your most intimate moments, my average reader, do you not rely on large cards held beyond the audience's sight? Have you ever applauded without being prompted by an illuminated sign?

THE PEOPLE'S REPUBLIC OF CHINA has launched a man into space. He claims the only man-made structure visible from the shuttle is the Great Wall. What about the Kansai International Airport (which is sinking)? The light from the Luxor Casino? What about smog? For *visible from space* read *in the eyes of God.*

THE PHENOMENA OF EXPERIENCE have been translated into understanding. Plug the exposed voids in the veneer cores to eliminate nesting. We live in the best of all possible worlds. Stain the compound to match the plywood finish.

THE AUTHOR EXPOSES HIMSELF IN PUBLIC like film. Every surface secretly desires to be ruled. A faint hazy cone in the plane of the ecliptic precedes the tabulation of a body by a train. Read only to resist the temptation to write. Skew lines and slickensides in an era of polarized light. The zip disk of snuff films your son defends as research has divided the community into infinite subdistances. Born losers born ready to be born again, we await the mayor's address in metal chairs. Then it hits me: I'm the mayor.

THE DOG IN THE CARTOON shoots a gun, overtakes the bullet in a car, and awaits it with an open mouth. Slight, continuous changes in the shapes of the scenery give the illusion of motion. In lieu of erections, sprouting cephalic contusions. Otherwise reduced to a pile of ash, the eyes of the mischievous cat remain, blinking. Contiguity substituted for substitution: flatten the duck with a frying pan and he becomes a frying pan. The bear indifferently fingers the holes in his chest. The giant ham around which the episode is organized weighs nothing, appears slippery, and is ultimately swallowed by a mouse. The popular breakfast sandwich is made of cartoon flesh. The child actor who worked opposite the dragon is scarred for life. Open your eyes. You're still holding the dynamite.

NO MATTER HOW BIG YOU MAKE A TOY, a child will find a way to put it in his mouth. There is scarcely a piece of playground equipment that has not been inside a child's mouth. However, the object responsible for the greatest number of choking deaths, for adults as well as children, is the red balloon. Last year alone, every American choked to death on a red balloon.

NERVOUS EXHAUSTION FROM PROLONGED FLIGHT cannot excuse her coloring. Nor that she was blinded at birth with a hot wire to increase the beauty of her singing. A culture that lacks a concept of lack remains foreign, no matter the quantity of aid, the quantity of coverage. What do the homeless say in lieu of *Get out?* One day we will all be landed. Remaining sensate into a late stage of decomposition, aka abstraction. Delivering supplies from the air is no problem. But to the air?

A WALL IS TORN DOWN to expand the room and we grow distant. At the reception, cookies left over from the intervention. In the era before the flood, you could speak in the second person. Now the skylighted forecourt is filled with plainclothesmen. I would like to draw your attention. Like a pistol? In the sense of a sketch? Both, she said, emphasizing nothing, if not emphasis. Squint, and the room dissolves into manageable triangles. Close your eyes completely and it reappears.

BEFORE THE INVENTION OF MOVIES, nobody moved. Rain like a curtain of beads. Snow like the absence of snow. Quit putting your mouth in my words, I said to the officer, before falling into his arms. Love of the uniform in lieu of uniform love. Lower your voice in a church, decrease your font in a poem. Not a sword suspended by a hair, but a mine triggered by a wire. At midnight, the question turns rhetorical. Does invention have a father? In an age of mechanical reproduction, is any sin original?

TO BUILD THE WORLD'S BIGGEST MIRROR, to outdate the moon, to dream en masse, to sleepmarch, to watch earthrise from the anonymous depths of our diamond helmets, screams Hamsun, and the general will will fall to the earth as highly stylized debris. For all that remains of the public are its enemies, whose image will not be returned, so let them eat astronaut ice cream, from which we have abstracted ice, let them read magazine verse in the waiting rooms of plastic surgeons commissioned to implant breasts into their brains. To pave the horizon with silver nitrate, to simulate the nation through reflected light, to watch over ourselves in our sleep, to experience mediacy immediately, screams Hamsun, raising his glass, by waking into a single dream, THE STATE.

A LARGE GROUP OF PICNICKING CHILDREN is struck by lightning. Four girls and four dogs are killed. Twenty-three children suffer burns, cataracts, macular holes, tympanic membrane rupture, and skull fracture. At the church service, the pastor organizes his eulogy around the trope of being called. God reached down with a finger of light, etc. But the positive charge originated in the ground and climbed an invisible ladder of electrons skyward.

THE PROSE IS DENSER than the plot, which pushes the plot to the surface. Walking around the hospital saying, People, we can do this. The style is rubbing off. Chicken again, or a satisfactory print thereof. It's amazing what we've accomplished, considering we're locked in the bathroom. It's OK to laugh. They can't hear you. Can you hear me? See: nothing.

THE ARTIST PROPOSES A SERIES OF LIGHTS attached to tall poles, spaced at intervals along our public roads, and illuminated from dusk to dawn. The public is outraged. The law's long arm cannot support its heavy hand. The public is outrage. Kindergartners simulate bayonet fighting with the common domestic fowl. Does this blood look good on me? Does this blood make me look fat? If you replace a cow's stomach with glass, don't complain when you cut your mouth.

READING IS IMPORTANT because it makes you look down, an expression of shame. When the page is shifted to a vertical plane, it becomes an advertisement, decree, and/or image of a missing pet or child. We say that texts displayed vertically are addressed to the public, while in fact, by failing to teach us the humility a common life requires, they convene a narcissistic mass. When you window-shop, when you shatter a store window, you see your own image in the glass.

WHEN NIGHT FALLS IN THE MIDDLE WEST we divide the multiple fruit of the pig. A drunk man calls out for traditional shepherds' music addressing the theme of love, scratch that, the theme of boredom. The children are made to recite the Office of the Shutting of the Eyes. The saltshaker is full of pepper. The peppershaker: glitter. At the bottom of every drained pool, there I are. There we am, openmouthed, awaiting the small, angular rain. A drunk man brews a second cup, one for each fist. Great tufts of white carpet pulled out in grief, scratch that, in boredom. In the planar region bounded by our counterglow, no means no. So does yes. Everything we own is designed to be easily washed, unlike the aprons of the butchers that we are.

WE DREAM OF RAIN that, in lieu of falling, moves parallel to the earth. Sheet after sheet of rain. Then an upward rain that originates a few feet off the ground. You can get under the rain and watch. With the disappearance of public space, we dream a rain that's moved indoors. A miniaturized rain restricted to one room, one wall, a box. Then we dream snow.

ONE WHO WOULD PURSUE a career as an assistant cannot be picky about what or whom she assists. Even the luckiest among us will spend years looking up precedents. In this we are ourselves assisted, usually by men who know nothing of surveying and have no tools. Shovel snow from the path; file snow under snow. We pursue our terminal degrees while watching somebody else's kids. The law student chases around the usher's wife. The inspector laughs because you're laughing. Not having read the author in question is no defense against the charge of plagiarism. Our boss is the hushed tone in which we discuss him.

THE PUBLIC DEPENDS upon private sorrow. Well-regulated peacetime sorrow. I respect no office founded before the invention of the pistol, before an emphasis on brushstroke. We decide on a motion. The body vetoes. Nostalgia is futurity's privileged form in this economy of downturns. Is the television a linear descendant of the musket or the hearth? In American motels, the lamps are nailed down so that you will want to steal them, a Christian notion. Get off my property, she says, when I try to calm her down. Get out of my car, she says, when I try to wake her up. We stop our rotten teeth with gold. We drink a crystal cola. We counteract unwanted odor at inestimable human cost. As if you could choose between loving and leaving the weather. The rich kids in Providence are moving to Mexico. Rich kids in Mexico are moving to Providence. I'm on my umpteenth Pabst, awaiting order, making difference.

RETURNING ASTRONAUTS almost always fall into a deep depression. They are stricken with an uncontrollable desire to gain weight. At dusk you will see them circling the park in silk pajamas, mocked by children, trailed by dogs. Prolonged weightlessness destroys the bones, the muscles, and, eventually, the larynx, which is why when astronauts return to earth we find that their speech has been reduced to a kind of quiet piping, at once soft and shrill, that is intelligible only to other astronauts, a piping that approaches, but is not, despite the government's assertions, song.

IF IT HANGS FROM THE WALL, it's a painting. If it rests on the floor, it's a sculpture. If it's very big or very small, it's conceptual. If it forms part of the wall, if it forms part of the floor, it's architecture. If you have to buy a ticket, it's modern. If you are already inside it and you have to pay to get out of it, it's more modern. If you can be inside it without paying, it's a trap. If it moves, it's outmoded. If you have to look up, it's religious. If you have to look down, it's realistic. If it's been sold, it's site-specific. If, in order to see it, you have to pass through a metal detector, it's public.

WE ARE A MEAN AND STUPID PEOPLE, but not without smooth muscle. When we get offended, we say, What's the big idea. The rest of the time we don't worry about it. Instead of national genius, a native lyric twined around the latticework of grammar. The bees we sent to space stopped making honey. Like a grown man, the monkeys wept. The night the shuttle crumbled on reentry, you were allowed to hug anybody you could find. We just stretched out on the beach. Best night of our lives.

A WELL-PLACED BLOW TO THE TEMPLE and it's 1986 in aeternum. Like a kid in a candy store crossed with a bull in a china shop, a depressive in a garage. After your uncle hooks you up, a sudden inability to recall where you got your doctorate, let alone in what. Walking around the basement asking, Whose blood is this? Not the beauty of the bottle rocket, but its justice. The infinite sympathy of breakaway glass. Bro, you said that already. Another summer spent searching for something to nurse back to health. Finding yourself.

THE GIRL PLAYS with nonrepresentational dolls. Her games are devoid of any narrative content, amusements that depend upon their own intrinsic form. If you make her a present of a toy, she will discard it and play with the box. And yet she will only play with a box that once contained a toy. Her favorite toy was a notion about color. She lost it in the snow.

THE DETECTIVE pushes red tacks into the map to indicate where bodies have been found. The shooter is aware of this practice and begins to arrange the bodies, and thus the tacks, into a pattern that resembles a smiley face. The shooter intends to mock the detective, who he knows will be forced to confront this pattern daily on the precinct wall. However, the formal demands of the smiley face increasingly limit the shooter's area of operation. The detective knows, and the shooter knows the detective knows, that the shooter must complete the upward curving of the mouth. The detective patrols the area of the town in which bodies must be found if the shooter is to realize his project. The plane on which the killings are represented, and the plane on which the killings take place, have merged in the minds of the detective and the shooter. The shooter dreams of pushing a red tack into the map, not of putting a bullet into a body. The detective begins to conceive of the town as a representation of the map. He drives metal stakes into the ground to indicate the tacks.

WE WORK IN ACCOUNTING for taste. True, Mallarmé wasted a lot of paper, but less than your average American. Liner notes eclipse the music, like eating the rind and discarding the flesh. How many Indians remain on the fence, they asked her, to see if she were gifted, then locked her in the closet with a carton of smokes. From the land's natural depressions arises the affect of home. Where the lines break of their own accord. Where shockwaves pulverize our stones. Let the machine get it, she was wont to say, when we didn't have a phone.

THE CAMERA WAS DISCOVERED before painting was invented. The first paintings were made on the inside walls of cameras. Still, painting was the first medium to attain a verisimilitude capable of confusing birds, the highest achievement in any art. When Wu Daozi painted dragons, their fins stirred. The rest of the story is about flatness. One-sided surfaces. A skin that speaks a vocabulary of rights. To explore color, we realized, leave it out. Like exchanging genius for its stroke. The bald girl is interested in boredom. I'm interested in algal cells and fungal hyphae. Our grant is awarded in installments of cigarettes. We are trying too hard not to be funny.

THE GOOD AND EVIL, THE BEAUTIFUL AND UGLY, have been assumed under the rubric of the interesting. Non sequitur rendered lyric by a retrospective act of will. Tongue worries tooth. Repetition worries referent. Non sequitur rendered will by a retrospective act of lyric.

HIDEAWAY BEDS were not invented to maximize space, but to conceal the unseemly reality of prostration. Thomas Jefferson, who held the first United States patent on a hideaway bed, devised a system of elevating and securing the bed to the ceiling. Each night the bed would be lowered slowly, and with great ceremony, thereby associating the animal fact of sleep with the plane of the divine. The contemporary hideaway bed, which is stored vertically, has snapped shut and killed at least ten businessmen. Most people can be trained to sleep standing up, to sleep with their eyes open, to somniloquize, to somnambulate. Mobilizing this tremendous dormant workforce is an ancient dream. Astronauts sleep strapped to their beds, like lunatics, like the lunatics they are.

PEOPLE WITH ALL MANNER OF PHOBIA, a fear of heights or crowds or marketplaces, public speaking or blood or prime numbers, have been known to overcome their panic by wearing glasses, not with corrective lenses, but with lenses of plain shatterproof plastic, which not only impose a mediate plane between them and the object of their fear, but apply a comforting pressure to the bridge of the nose. When you encounter a person seized by terror, softly squeeze this bony structure, and he will be instantaneously subdued. In an age of contact lenses and laser surgery, it is safe to assume that a person who persists in wearing glasses is undergoing treatment.

A BACHELOR made from a cake of shaving soap and a tin of dentifrice, pursued by an admiring throng of whiskers and teeth, announces a willful deadness of surface called *publicity.* The animate talks back to the animator, blowing his cover as delicately as glass. A poorly painted explosion either resembles a bunch of flowers (static) or a nosebleed (overly rich in color); the brushstroke itself must be made to mime the direction of the pressure. When our story opens, gas begins to stream. The crowd yawns with wonder. History, screams Hamsun, the junior senator from Wisconsin, will vindicate my mustache. When a vanguard in bowlers mows down a vanguard in tarbooshes, you've reached modernity; leave a message at the beep.

LASER TECHNOLOGY has fulfilled our people's ancient dream of a blade so fine that the person it cuts in half remains standing and alive until he moves and cleaves. Until we move, none of us can be sure that we have not already been cut in half, or in many pieces, by a blade of light. It is safest to assume that our throats have already been slit, that the slightest alteration in our postures will cause the painless severance of our heads.

A SIDE OF BEEF ON A SILVER PLATTER, a slice of life on a silver screen. A beast with two backs, a war with two fronts. *Búsqueda en Google* an Abraham doll with realistic trembling. Her exit is emphasized by the receding lines of the parquet floor—who says art criticism is impractical? I'll grant the world doesn't need another novel, if you'll grant the novel doesn't need another world. The smugness masks a higher sadness, a sudden chiasmic reversal mistaken for love. I just want to be held, but contingently, the way the mind holds a trauma that failed to take place. Realistic suction, realism sucks. Ah, Bartleby!

III

DIDACTIC ELEGY

Sense that sees itself is spirit

Novalis

Intention draws a bold, black line across an otherwise white field.
Speculation establishes gradations of darkness
where there are none, allowing the critic to posit narrative time.
I posit the critic to distance myself from intention, a despicable affect.
Yet intention is necessary if the field is to be understood as an economy.

By *economy* I mean that the field is apprehension in its idle form.
The eye constitutes any disturbance in the field as an object.
This is the grammatical function of the eye. To distinguish between objects,
the eye assigns value where there is none.

When there is only one object the eye is anxious.
Anxiety here is comic; it provokes amusement in the body.
The critic experiences amusement as a financial return.

It is easy to apply a continuous black mark to the surface of a primed canvas.
It is difficult to perceive the marks without assigning them value.
The critic argues that this difficulty itself is the subject of the drawing.
Perhaps, but to speak here of a subject is to risk affirming
intention where there is none.

It is no argument that the critic knows the artist personally.
Even if the artist is a known quantity, interpretation is an open struggle.
An artwork aware of this struggle is charged with negativity.
And yet naming negativity destroys it.
Can this process be made the subject of a poem?

No,
but it can be made the object of a poem.
Just as the violation of the line amplifies the whiteness of the field,
so a poem can seek out a figure of its own impossibility.
But when the meaning of such a figure becomes fixed, it is a mere positivity.

Events extraneous to the work, however, can unfix the meaning of its figures,
thereby recharging it negatively. For example,
if airplanes crash into towers and those towers collapse,
there is an ensuing reassignment of value.
Those works of art enduringly susceptible to radical revaluations are
      masterpieces.
The phrase *unfinished masterpiece* is redundant.

Now the critic feels a new anxiety in the presence of the drawing.
Anxiety here is tragic; it inspires a feeling of irrelevance.
The critic experiences irrelevance as a loss of capital.

To the critic, the black line has become simply a black line.
What was once a gesture of negativity has lost its capacity to refer
to the difficulties inherent in reference.
Can this process be made the subject of a poem?

No,
but a poem may prefigure its own irrelevance,
thereby staying relevant
despite the transpiration of extraneous events.

This poem will lose its relevance if and when there is a significant resurgence
of confidence in the function of the artwork.
If artworks are no longer required to account for their own status,
this poem's figures will then be fixed and meaningless.

But meaninglessness, when accepted, can be beautiful
in the way the Greeks were beautiful
when they accepted death.
Only in this sense can a poem be heroic.
After the towers collapsed

many men and women were described as heroes.
The first men and women described as heroes were in the towers.
To call them heroes, however, implies that they were willing to accept their
   deaths.
But then why did some men and women
jump from the towers as the towers collapsed?
One man, captured on tape, flapped his arms as he fell.

Rescue workers who died attempting to save the men and women trapped in the
   towers are, in fact, heroes,
but the meaning of their deaths is susceptible to radical revaluation.
The hero makes a masterpiece of dying
and even if the hero is a known quantity
there is an open struggle over the meaning of her death. According to the
   president,

any American who continues her life as if the towers had not collapsed
is a hero. This is to conflate the negative with the counterfactual.
The president's statement is meaningless
unless to be American means to embrace one's death,
which is possible.

It is difficult to differentiate between the collapse of the towers
and the image of the towers collapsing.
The influence of images is often stronger than the influence of events,
as the film of Pollock painting is more influential than Pollock's paintings.

But as it is repeated, the power of an image diminishes,
producing anxiety and a symbolic reinvestment.
The image may then be assigned value where there is none.
Can an image be heroic?

No,
but an image may proclaim its distance from the event it ostensibly depicts;
that is, it may declare itself its own event,
and thereby ban all further investment.

The critic watches the image of the towers collapsing.
She remembers less and less about the towers collapsing
each time she watches the image of the towers collapsing.

The critic feels guilty viewing the image like a work of art,
but guilt here stems from an error of cognition,
as the critic fails to distinguish between an event
and the event of the event's image.

The image of the towers collapsing is a work of art
and, like all works of art, may be rejected
for soiling that which it ostensibly depicts. As a general rule,
if a representation of the towers collapsing
may be repeated, it is unrealistic.

Formalism is the belief that the eye does violence to the object it apprehends.
All formalisms are therefore sad.
A negative formalism acknowledges the violence intrinsic to its method.
Formalism is therefore a practice, not an essence.

For example, a syllogism subjected to a system of substitutions
allows us to apprehend the experience of logic
at logic's expense.

Negative formalisms catalyze an experience of structure.
The experience of structure is sad,
but, by revealing the contingency of content,
it authorizes hope.

This is the role of the artwork—to authorize hope,
but the very condition of possibility for this hope is the impossibility of its
        fulfillment.
The value of hope is that it has no use value.
Hope is the saddest of formalisms.

The critic's gaze is a polemic without object
and only seeks a surface
upon which to unfold its own internal contradictions.
Conditions permitting, a drawing might then be significant,
but only as a function of her search for significance.

It is not that the significance is mere appearance.
The significance is real but impermanent.
Indeed, the mere appearance of significance is significant.
We call it *politics*.

The lyric is a stellar condition.
The relation between the lyric I and the lyric poem
is like the relation between a star and starlight.
The poem and the I are never identical and their distance may be measured in
        time.
Some lyric poems become visible long after their origins have ceased to exist.

The heavens are anachronistic. Similarly, the lyric
lags behind the subjectivity it aspires to express. Expressing this disconnect
is the task of the negative lyric,
which does not exist.

If and when the negative lyric exists, it will be repetitious.
It will be designed to collapse in advance, producing an image
that transmits the impossibility of transmission. This familiar gesture,
like a bold black stroke against a white field,
will emphasize flatness, which is a failure of emphasis.

The critic repeats herself for emphasis.
But, since repetition emphasizes only the failure of sense,
this is a contradiction.
When contradictions are intended they grow lyrical
and the absence of the I is felt as a presence.

If and when the negative lyric exists, it will affect a flatness
to no effect.
The failure of flatness will be an expression of depth.

Towers collapse didactically.
When a tower collapses in practice it also collapses in theory.
Brief dynamic events then carry meanings
that demand memorials,
vertical memorials at peace with negativity.

Should we memorialize the towers or the towers' collapse?
Can any memorial improve on the elegance of absence?
Or perhaps, in memoriam, we should destroy something else.

I think that we should draw a bold, black line across an otherwise white field
and keep discussion of its meaning to a minimum.
If we can close the event to further interpretation
we can keep the collapse from becoming a masterpiece.

The key is to intend as little as possible in the act of memorialization.
By intending as little as possible we refuse to assign value where there is none.
Violence is not yet modern; it fails to acknowledge the limitations of its
       medium.
When violence becomes aware of its mediacy and loses its object
it will begin to resemble love.
Love is negative because it dissolves
all particulars into an experience of form.
Refusing to assign meaning to an event is to interpret it lovingly.

The meaninglessness of the drawing is therefore meaningful
and the failure to seek out value is heroic.
Is this all that remains of poetry?

Ignorance that sees itself is elegy.

IV

ANGLE OF YAW

THE DARK CROWD CANNOT BE SEEN DIRECTLY, the dark crowd does not interact with light, but the dark crowd can be detected by measuring its gravitational effects on visible crowds. The visible crowd moves toward the dark crowd, as insects toward a blacklight trap, in the tropism we call *history*. Riot guns with rubber bullets, tear gas, water cannons, flying wedges of heavily armored police, are not only incapable of dispersing the dark crowd, but, by inciting a phase change in the visible crowd, expand its ranks.

SEEN FROM ABOVE, exposition, climax, and denouement all take place at once. God sees the future as we see the past: through a trimetrogon. In the name of the camera, the film, and the view itself. Simultaneous eternities are superimposed to create the illusion of plenitude, but the transposition of planes is a poor substitute for the transmigration of souls. I think Andrei Rublev says, *Nothing is as terrible as snow falling in a temple,* because without a distinction between inside and outside, there can be no extra-temporal redemption. That, and how anybody can just lie down and make an angel, even a Tartar. Even an angel.

A PERSON IS PHOBIC, that is, mentally imbalanced, when his fears fail to cancel out his other fears. The healthy, too, are terrified of heights, but equally terrified of depths, as terrified of dark as light, open spaces as closed. The phobic are overbold, not overly apprehensive, and must be conditioned to fear the opposite of what they fear. The difficulty of such a treatment lies in finding the counterbalancing terror. What is the opposite of a marketplace? A prime number? Blood? A spider?

TALK ME DOWN, MAN, TALK ME DOWN. Obsessive repetition of meaningless gestures. A dangerous level of light in the blood. The caller claims to have discovered the imprint of a trilobite embedded in the sky. It's the kind of thing, he says, that makes you pray to God. That you might live forever. In these several states of shock. At what point in the conversation did you realize her breathing had stopped? When I kissed her. But there's no time for this. The black helicopters are upon us, our daughters flee from the house, weeping, crazy with joy.

AN IMAGE OF ULTIMACY in an age of polarized light. Will you marry me, skywrites the uncle. A pill to induce awe with a side effect of labor. A lateral inward tilting and the aircraft pushes its envelope. A minor innovation in steering outdates a branch of literature. Envelopes push back. The way a wake turns to ice, then vapor, then paper, uniting our analogues in error, intimacy's highest form. Jet engines are designed to sublimate stray birds. *No* appears in the corn.

THE THIRD DIVISION OF A RUMINANT'S STOMACH is called a *psalterium* because, when slit open, its folds fall apart like the leaves of a book. The fruit is star-shaped when cut in cross section and is therefore called *star fruit*. Our people often name an object after the manner in which we destroy it.

THE VIEWING PUBLIC DEMANDS an image of itself. The revelation of a telltale trope. The evidence is against us, rubbing. Heat from the right margin reduces the sentence. Light, dry, explosive snow. The pianist is remembered for his influential humming over what is considered a poor rendition. Of radical emotional incapacitation. Of opaque, damp permutation. At what point did you kick away the ladder? In chapter four, where the reader is encouraged to look down from above. Where the author, posing as a question, opens up the floor.

I BELIEVE THERE IS A QUESTION IN THE BACK. Yes, thank you. Do you own Hitler's upper teeth? If you do own Hitler's upper teeth, and it seems that you do, would you be able to resist the temptation to try them on? If you're wearing Hitler's upper teeth right now, and it seems that you are, how does that effect the validity of your answer? What if you write your answer? If you tell me you love me while wearing Hitler's upper teeth, should I believe you? Is it wrong to be kissed by a person wearing Hitler's upper teeth? What if the person wearing the teeth is Jewish, a rabbi even? Can we put a dollar figure on the upper teeth of Hitler? Are the upper teeth of every German in some important sense the upper teeth of Hitler? Would it be a good or bad thing for German children to be forced to try on the upper teeth of Hitler? And if it would be a good thing, and I think we can all agree that it would, is that because they would learn that these teeth are somehow exceptional, maybe even supernatural, or because they would realize that Hitler's upper teeth are composed of a soft pulp core surrounded by a layer of hard dentin coated with enamel— just plain old teeth? Can Hitler's upper teeth ever be forgiven? And, if so, all at once?

ONE IF BY LAND, TWO IF BY SEA, sings the canary. Warning: coloration. The very existence of concealed space constitutes an ambush. An abrupt change in sentence structure turns our fire friendly. Our response is calculated to make a false alarm come true, a true alarm come false. There is no describing a weapon that spreads white space.

WOMEN HAVE NO DESIRE to travel in outer space. When men have forced women to travel in outer space, the results have been disastrous. If you mention space travel to a woman, she will say, Don't even go there, she will say, You can't go home again, she will say, Been there, done that. That there is more space inside one small woman than in all of heaven has been verified experimentally. She will say, Have I gained weight, she will say, I no longer love you and/or I'm not sure I ever loved you, she will say, Most theorists believe the universe is flat. The first woman in space is still there.

DEAR CYRUS, HE PUTS DOWN, DEAR CYRUS, what you experience as an inconsistency in tone, is, in fact, the Montessori method, in which we practice abstinence during the period of ovulation, in which we move across the plane of fracture, where adjacent surfaces are differentially displaced. Dear Personified Abstraction, he puts down, Dear Counterstain with Safranine, I am writing to describe a perfect circle, the sudden sine curve of a fleeing deer, and to request your absence at my table, with quakes of lesser magnitude to follow. Dear Reader, he puts down, Dear He Puts Down, when the golden parachute failed to decelerate your cousin, the Baron, the first dog in space, the kids fanned out across the field and screamed *I've got it,* mistaking the shower of sparks for bedtime, the luminous obligate parasites for a lecture on film. Dear Lerner, he puts down, Earth to Lerner, throw three damn strikes and get us out of this sentence, but the runner had long since grown into his base.

CHILD ACTORS are not children, that much we know. Their reputation for viciousness is, by all accounts, deserved. Napoleon and Liszt were child actors. In situation comedies, child actors are black. Some child actors have never been off-camera. If you build a set and start filming, a child actor will come downstairs. Some doctors believe it is the constant surveillance that stunts the growth of the child actor, the pressure of the viewing public's gaze, while in fact a child actor off-camera is like a fish out of water. He cannot breathe.

WE HAVE ASSEMBLED for the athletic contest in tiered seats. Once, we assembled in a central core with mobile spiral arms. Or, lying on our backs, we formed a radiating cluster, imposing animal figures and names upon the stars. Now we watch heavily armored professionals assume formations on a grid of artificial grass. Wishbone. Shotgun. Power I.

WE CAN FEEL THE CHANGING of the tense. The sky distends six inches. Like a parachute opening inside the body. If you don't secure your own mask first, you'll just sit there stroking the child's hair. In the dream you form part of the wreckage you pick through: an allegory of reading. Who knows how many hijackers have been foiled by an engrossing in-flight movie. This one seems to be about symmetry, about getting yours. Its simplified geometrical forms recall the landscapes of our simulators. It's not just the pilots who have to be trained. When you ask the stewardess for another tiny bottle, she says, This is neither a time nor a place.

PHOTOGRAPHED FROM ABOVE, the shadows of the soldiers seem to stand upright, casting bodies. Birds are rarely depicted from a bird's-eye view. From this angle, she doesn't love me. Half light, half ideology. Each of us is impressed as pixels into an ad for democracy. Give the people what they want, says the TV. A powerful suction effect? Extra-extra-cheese? The sixth sense, the sense with which we read, is the ability to perceive the loss of other senses; we have lost this sense.

THE SMUGNESS MASKS A HIGHER SADNESS. We are unaware of the patterns we generate. In the carpet grass, the snow crust. When we don't know a word, we say, Look it up. Up? And the Lord withdrew his thumb, trailing delicate, rootlike filaments, leaving a hole in my chest the size of a polis. From which I address you, Hamsun. If you dig deep enough, you hit water, then hell, then China. So why not fly? Getting there is half the fun; the other half: not getting there.

A SUDDEN EXPERIENCE OF STRUCTURE and the heart gives out. He checks himself in. Lies on the window and looks out the bed. The sense of having said it before keeps him, again and again, from beginning. As the belief that the respirator is powered by the rain keeps him breathing. The outlet is inhabited by a family of mice who also regard their home as a source of power. He shuts his eyes to see himself from above. He shuts his eyes so tightly they recoil. To be forced to drink water is an ancient form of torture, older than being denied water. That the body eats itself is neither here nor there. With what exceeds description we busy ourselves.

THIS IS NOT YOUR FATHER'S BOREDOM. 1986: the year in pictures, the year in tears. Out of the ordinary emerged the first, doomed shoots. In my honor they will one day name and electrify a chair. Wind in my hair, windshield in my teeth. A grammar derived for an early death. Mere wit is the new wailing; black, the new black. My best friend went to Mexico and all I got was this lousy elegy. As easy as taking context from a baby. I'd like to say a few words in memory of Memory, an all-state wrestler who left teeth-marks on the median. I can't help feeling that it should have been me. It was, whispers the priest.

AS LONG AS THE BREATH LASTS, the vowel can be prolonged. The name refers both to the field of play and the game itself, in which you can utilize any part of the body save the brain. A flat, affected tone is sweeping the nation. We sincerely hope we will never have to use the cables strung to the scenery, but it's nice to know they're there.

A STUDY OF A CHILD [ERASED], a study of erasure [Child], the swiftness of pencils repeating a theme until it achieves the illusion of enterable space. Rake me, she said, with a moral light, but the luster of her ostrich-feather fan had dimmed her eyes. For the purposes of study, we have removed those figures attributed to disciples, yielding a string of visual commas and the inscription *Turn away.* We work with a found vocabulary, working backwards from the detail to the richly textured blindness of Parmigianino's gaze. Anyway, as a child, I was thrown from my Powell Peralta, and when I came to, my left-brain had been erased. No street, no land, no sky—just scape.

WE ARE PLEASED TO OFFER A LAMP that turns on and off when you clap, when you clap your eyes. A lamp that lets you see in the dark without disturbing the dark. A lamp producing natural light. A lamp that when you clap turns on and on.

IN THE COMMERCIAL she just stabs a straw into an orange and sucks. We tried that at home and lost massive amounts of blood. When I was little, she confessed, beginning to cry, we were forced to race in sacks, to race in pairs with our near legs bound. Coach was finally fired for rewarding each good hit with a sparkling article of porn. His slow-pitch team was sponsored by AA. His house was always already egged. It was when I tried to eat a straw through a straw that I learned my first important lesson about form.

WHEN WE FOUND EYES in the hospital Dumpster, we decided to build the most awesome snowman ever. The author addresses the reader; the clown, the kids at home. Angels are absences in the snow, visible only from above. When it thaws they will stand up and search for the children they have known.

THE ROSE has a minutely serrate margin, like a poem. There ends analogy. A dying process. At the border of the cornea and sclera, a momentary wavering. Excluded from beatific vision, but not condemned to further punishment. In the dream she told me she felt fine. Like dust. To what shall we liken analogy, if not to hypermetropia. These carpets are the color of migraine. Note to self: change your life. I assume the palmate antlers of hoofed mammals have so often been likened to candelabra I'm not even going to try. Boy, you got trouble in your head. Every time, he says, breasts are described in the poems of men, a woman undergoes mastectomy. I said *he says* to gain some credibility, which is a privileged form of distance. This one goes out to Grandma Elsie, short for Elsewhere, whom I never met. This one goes out to Grandma Rosie, who couldn't remember her first cancer by the time she died of being ready. Her ashes are on a shelf in Cambridge. Awaiting scattering. Note to self: don't publish this. Besides the half-dead and their families, everybody in the home was from the Indies. Carpets the color of. We administered music and morphine. For ninety-four years, she had performed her gender admirably. Anyway, this isn't a time or a place. But the day she died some punk nearly hit me with his bike, parked it, and got all in my face. Boy, you got trouble in your head. I started to cry. Like a woman, he said. As if to give me strength.

WE BEG THE QUESTION that gives the lie. Which swallows the usage. Half of the panel supports the sentence: Without emotion. We pursue a color of maximum lightness. Town crier become town drunk. A diet of bacon and meth. Prolonged speech making to delay the action. Of the hammer. Convicted on the strength of his indifference to conviction. The music is inadmissible. The gavel fell on a percussion cap and now we're holding candles, singing, My God, My God, show me what you're working with.

RAPIDLY REPEATED STIMULI have locked our jaws and fixed our gazes upward. Public launches are designed to trick the body into an attitude of prayer. Despair is an oculogyric crisis, as every politician knows, and can be treated with displays of strength in the upper air. Perhaps scratching out one's eyes is all that remains of bearing witness, but note the hegemony of the image among the blind. The way our national uncle stares from the poster, claiming to want every passerby. *Nunc dimittis servum tuum,* you murderers. I come from a long line of prematurely balding communards who would prefer not to. Keep your infernal, infertile high ground, with its toll roads of crushed glass.

A GREAT BOOK must be frozen and fractured along its faults in order to lay bare internal structure. Anna Karenina touches the paperknife to her cheek. When a child dies in a novel, he enters the world. And writes the novel. The calories in a great book equal those burned in its reading. Or its burning. Even if there are no great books, argues Levin, we must act as if there were. For the sake of the peasants who work the paper. A gentleman may fight duels only with other gentlemen. A reader may not demand satisfaction.

A BRIEF, COLLECTIVE SHUDDER and the desire passed into its opposite. The public shared a cigarette. Now to choose between loving our offspring and loving offspring in general, between veiling the reference and taking the vow. The right to have it both ways is inalienable or it isn't. You can't have it both ways. A contradiction shifting planes produces lightning. Or a reflection of distant lightning in the clouds.

THE MAN OBSERVES THE ACTION ON THE FIELD with the tiny television he brought to the stadium. He is topless, painted gold, bewigged. His exaggerated foam index finger indicates the giant screen upon which his own image is now displayed, a model of fanaticism. He watches the image of his watching the image on his portable TV on his portable TV. He suddenly stands with arms upraised and initiates the wave that will consume him.

EQUIPPED WITH FLUFFY PLUMAGE that allows for almost noiseless flight. Our bombs are dropped from such altitudes our wars have ended by the time they reach their targets. Like that sentence. No, like any sentence. Maintaining the blood supply to the brain during rapid vertical acceleration requires subtle reasoning, soft music. Hence an earphone in the helmet. What goes up, must come down, pleads the child of the astronaut. Not if you go way, way up.

A SURGERY TO ABRIDGE the body. A reader-friendly body presented to the public. The public depends from a well-regulated militia. Our army, too, has its required reading. A soldier must read Tolstoy's *War* (abr.), Dostoyevsky's *Crime* (abr.). Even in death, the old debate between depth and surface: some poets attach weights to their ankles, others just float facedown. What is the value of reading? Depends. What is it keeping you from doing?

AN INFINITE PROGRESSION OF FINAL FRONTIERS designed to distract the public from its chest wound. We will not just sit here being mooned, insists the president. Your kids are arranging a day of national mourning with a trunk full of tequila and pipe bombs. In despair, the painter returns to the figure. Or has the world grown abstract? In my experience, the eyeball hardens. In my opinion, the sound of weeping. Maybe the microphone itself is speaking. On the count of three, everyone everywhere concede everything.

THE INHERENT DIFFICULTY OF THE GAME rests exclusively in the obscurity of its object. Points are taken away for killing civilians, but points are irrelevant. Gold earns you extra men. Children, if questioned, deny the mediation of the joystick or fail to hear the question. Often we are permitted to return to levels we've surpassed to search for mushrooms.

THE TIME-RELEASE SEDATIVE is advertised by means of accelerated photographic frames. The music fails to produce conscious awareness but evokes a violent response. As an artist I'm interested in filling things with blood, especially clocks, but as a mom I demand the illusion of continuous motion. Best viewed through radial slits in a drum. Best viewed before 1987. A flickering series of stills induced by a stroke in turn induces a stroke, restoring the illusion of continuous perceptual flow. My colleagues, what have we learned? That consciousness has a neural correlate in snow. That movement is painted on.

SHE HAS TAPED AN AERIAL PHOTOGRAPH of our neighborhood to the ceiling. She looks up to see our house from above while we're in bed. This is but one example of her uncontrollable desire to look down on the structures that she's in.

AMERICANS HAVE CONQUERED THEIR FEAR of public speaking by abolishing the public. Chief among our exports: wisps of precipitation. Because it receives the impression of your teeth, it is genuine emotion. Compare the streak left on the gemstone with that left on the retina. Confusing the desire to display affection with affection, we applaud the veterans of an imaginary conflict with real victims. An immoderate reverence for tradition guides everything but our reading. I throw my own party and go away.

THE SOLDIER IN THE FILM asks the audience to describe his wounds. Unaware his legs are elsewhere, he attempts to walk out of the screen. What matters is the form, not the content, of the airdrop, how it alludes to manna. Then kill me, he begs. Active soldiers act like actors, inactive actors act like soldiers, audience members vomit in their giant sodas. Dance, I say, aiming near his feet. Think, I say, aiming near his head. The crowd dismembers. Now I'm on my back, making an angel, awaiting not the peanut butter and propaganda, but the flowering apparatus that retards its fall.

SPUN DOWN FROM AND REELED UP TO the hand by a flick of the wrist. In what sense is it a toy, she asks, if it catches real fish? Like soldiers carrying popguns and switchblade combs. At first, the elephant could fly only when he held a feather in his trunk. Would you rather live during the ascension of a civilization, asks the top-hatted cricket, or during its decline? Pygmalion or Pinocchio? Then he learned to hold it in his mind. Not every off-screen voice is the voice of God. But we must act as if it were. For the sake of the rabbit who has run out of landscape and plugged the shotgun with his finger. Do rabbits have fingers? I don't know, do chickens? The hunted confounds the hunter with a sudden change of gender.

THE TONE DOES TERRIBLE THINGS to the landscape. Its flatness drapes the landscape in unspeakable light, unspeakable space. The public, delicately inflamed, attempts to change the channel. But a channel cannot be changed by force. During the course of festive occasions, ash rains down. Bits of parti-colored ash inform us that our tone is festive. Perhaps change must come from within a channel, suggests Levin, from within a landscape draped with depth?

DEAR CYRUS, HE PUTS DOWN, DEAR REPETITION, while you were driving home from, how shall I put this, Mexico, driving dark pales into the panic grass, the kids got into the Roman candles, the ginger vodka, the Bible I gave your daughter was hollow, contained a, how shall I, pistol, two kinds of people in this world, do I smell incense, swimmers and nonswimmers, a child with puppy dog eyes asks if puppies go to heaven, the pistol proves untrainable, ruins the carpet, a no or no question, I guess I just assumed dogs dog-paddled, Dear, Dear, he puts down, Dear Me, when a dog drowns an angel gets its wings, and a long proboscis for sucking blood, no self-putdowns, she screamed, I pretended it was alive so I could pretend to put it to sleep, how shall I, sweetheart, no doggy heaven, put this, without a doggy hell.

HOLD ME, says the microphone. The dialogue inside my body is breaking down. The doctor insists on changing the tense, but the gesture is lost on me, stranded on the skin. When did I ever say that I could teach you how to live, demands the canvas. Light wishes only to be a history of its transfers, wishes only to be land. They have pricked my back with a series of suspected allergens, an allegory of reading, but my skin is notoriously indifferent. To print media. To the dialogue of fear and pity designed to restore the public's settings. You have a swelled head, complain my hands.

THE SUN SETS IN A WEAK SENSE, striking conjunctions of rock from the view, imparting a vivid red to the red to the red—the text is skipping. The author dreams of cutting an adjective and tucking it behind the reader's ear like a flower. And cutting *like a flower* and tucking it behind the reader's ear like a flower.

BORN NOSTALGIC, THE ARTIST PROPOSES a return to despair. He installs himself in your freezer. The critic argues it is not real hair, that real hair could never do this. At what point, asks the critic, did you realize the blood was fake? About halfway through the transfusion, when he began to talk a bunch of bullshit. About the formal capacity for choice? Yes, how did you know? I worked as an artist during the war.

THE AIRCRAFT ROTATES about its longitudinal axis, shifting the equinoxes slowly west. Our system of measure is anchored by the apparent daily motion of stars that no longer exist. When the reader comes to, the writer hits him again. Just in case God isn't dead, our astronauts carry sidearms. This is not your captain speaking, thinks the captain. A magnetic field reversal turns our fire friendly. Fleeing populations leave their bread unleavened, their lines unbroken.

WHEN WE SAW THE PATTERN, we took the kids out of school. Broke out the special water. Two churches linked by a sudden alley through the corn. As the Hopi myth foretells. A massive loss of technology. A spider leaves a string between two points. Think about it. From the duster it appears a thing of glory. Makes you reconsider the whole idea of property. Stems inside formations have blown nodes. Explain that, Mr. TV. Part of the confusion involves words. We wake up with mud on our feet. The other part is just the way we are. Scared of the new when it's thousands of years old. If you have never seen a sleeping toddler crawl beyond the lip of porch light, zip it. If my meaning is clear, it's already too late. For God's sake people. Open your hearts.

V

TWENTY-ONE GUN SALUTE
FOR RONALD REAGAN

I am wearing a Mikhail Gorbachev Halloween mask.

Blood is a vegetable when it forms part of a school lunch.

Tell the boys to go out there and win one for me.

The former president entered my room at night.

We celebrated by breaking off pieces of the wall.

I want the tone to have a very broad surface in relation to its depth.

I want a gun for protection.

      I want the form to enact the numbing it describes.

      I would shoot myself only in self-defense.

Pornography considered as a weapon system and v.v.

An accurate Civil War reenactment should include reinstating the draft.

The stigma attached to a diplomatically communicated disease.

It's important to talk to your readers about drugs.

The nipple is just visible under the anchorwoman's blouse.

This is your tax dollars hard at work.

I have deleted many beautiful lines.

      A highly accurate weapon housed in a silo.

      I can't stop crying.

I was drunk the night of the accident.

All the other painters were like, Why didn't I think of that?

I have agreed not to defend Poland from the east.

I have agreed not to defend Poland from the East.

Mom says we can keep it if we feed it.

Nightlights go out all over America.

Brutus is urging his comrades to seize a fleeting opportunity.

      We salivate at the sound of the bell.

      That part of the concept corresponding to the wrist

is slit, emitting music.
There go the conventions Dad gave his life to protect.
The Soviet director argued convincingly against the use of sound.
Characterized by alternating rigidity and extreme flexibility.
The president's legacy is speaking slowly.
An epistemology borrowed from game shows.
Love is made to highly realistic dolls.
  The passivity of dolphins has been wildly exaggerated.
  Abortion is murder.

A child could have painted that.
We dipped cicadas in WD-40 and ignited them with punks.
Magnetic resonance imaging reveals a degenerate hemisphere.
A diamond cheval-de-frise tops the White House.
The floral arrangement is based on outmoded ideology.
I am unmatched in my portrayal of subtle human emotions.
Workers report cracks in our mode.
  There is no beauty like the beauty of a throwaway line
  the split second before it's thrown.

We carried home the reader shoulder high.
I neither regret nor recall my presidency.
Carefully equilibrated parts designed to move in the breath.
It can easily be converted into a fully automatic.
Mikey likes it.
I prefer apostasy from the top down to belief from the bottom up.
You must cross four bases in a diamond pattern in order to score.
  The bang caused by the shockwave
  preceding an aircraft traveling at the speed of sound

is my middle name.

I am attempting to stress the absence of hope while implying resignation.

A trademark used in a figurative context and in lowercase.

Minute hooks fasten to a corresponding strip with a surface of uncut pile.

A moment of unprecedented clarity experienced as a loss.

The starlings nesting in the bell's flared opening

did not hear the toll that slew them.

  This is a masterpiece on a very grand scale.

  I have drastically relaxed the standards of sexual behavior.

The pathos is visible when you hold the poem to the light.

She comes twice a month, in the first and third quarters of the moon.

The Soviets have prevailed.

I am beloved for my hoarse voice, ample nose, and timeworn hat.

The silvery leaves change position at nightfall.

What if we start over underground?

I propose truth is reached by a continuing dialectic.

  I disagree.

  Your life isn't worth the paper it's printed on.

My practical designs include a 1934 Sears refrigerator

and the interiors of NASA spacecraft.

Infinite Mind; Spirit; Soul; Principle; Life; Truth; Love.

An ideal cage bird given the pronounced affection among mates.

I am fond of lightning without audible thunder.

Reach out and touch someone.

Even the most conservative among us have lost all faith

  in the possibility of evoking a common cultural framework.

  Nobody moves

and nobody gets hurt.
The stoatlike creature symbolizes guilt.
The meanings detonate at preset depths.
I have never felt like a real man.
The holocaust is advanced tentatively to test public reaction.
Weeping is substantially, but not technically,
an admission of wrongdoing.

> Flight attendant: Oh my God, Oh my God, Oh my—
> Control tower: Take deep breaths.

A quick search has turned up the appropriate affect.
I respect the silky detail of your still-life paintings.
If you had been hypnotized, silly, you wouldn't know it.
This way the reader can answer other incoming calls.
Proceeds from the arms sales were then funneled to the Contras.
They held my father down and shaved his beard.
America is the A-team among nations,

> bursting with energy, courage, and determination.
> May I put my tongue in your ear?

Never wake a sleepwalker.
The Orient has regained the lamp and we are doomed.
Such a process of repetition is called reduplication.
The passion to be reckoned upon is fear.
The audience hears the voice of an on-screen character
who is not seen speaking.
These angels will eat anything—demon, sparrow, angel.

> My ability to appeal to white Southerners
> has diminished considerably

since I posed nude in the pages of *Foreign Policy.*
My government dropped an aluminum soap of various fatty acids
on my pen pal and her family.
Why don't we blame the sinking on Spain?
Financial benefits accorded to big business will be passed down to consumers.
Reading is cool.
A little shadow enhances the memory.

> We conduct ourselves in a free and easy manner
> but at heart are false and cold.

"God Bless America" was memorably sung by Kate Smith.
They were married hours before their double suicide.
You never called me before I was famous.
The names of the dead are inscribed in the wall.
The play is making Hamlet's mother uncomfortable.
I can't feel my legs.
The limit of latitude past which trees will not grow.

> Tear down this wall.
> Let them eat snow.

Then, without warning, our guiding star burned out.
We stood around the sleeping infant to see if she was breathing.
The poet notes that beautiful days and seasons do not last.
My emergence from my mother was captured on film.
All I ask is that we stop executing the mentally handicapped.
The stadium lights prevent the cereus from blooming.
But what if the mentally handicapped want to be executed?

> Big Bird towers over the human actors.
> We have both the right and duty to expand

into the blasted lands of southwest Asia.
Let's add touches of ethnic instrumentation.
I am attracted to women I do not respect.
The child makes a substantial advancement in poetics
with a canister of hair spray and a Bic.
Then you wake up next to a war criminal.
A rapid slide through a series of consecutive tones.
>
> The memorial will have to be continuous.
> Lift every voice and sing.

Your brother told me he feels mostly dead on the inside.
The strings are damped by wood and metal.
Station signals, picked up by elevated antennas
are delivered by cable to the receivers of subscribers.
Sexual abstinence is a partial solution.
A vague but strong attraction draws me to Moscow.
The white prizefighter doesn't have a prayer.
>
> Entities should not be multiplied needlessly.
> I can get you a healthy baby for five hundred dollars.

It's a lot better if you take out the plot.
Silvered surfaces face the vacuum.
The nightingale filled the pauses between sobs.
Mechanically separated chicken parts.
Crocodiles weep to attract victims.
There are such moments in life, dear reader, such feelings…
One can but point to them—and pass them by.
>
> All that remains of pleasure is frottage.
> The clouds were sown with crystals of dry ice

to stimulate rain for the president's funeral.
Private-sector affluence, public-sector squalor.
The hostage is growing romantically attached to her captor.
Jesus likes me.
My visit to the dermatologist possessed a nightmarish quality.
Mercy, the speaker is instructing Shylock, must be given freely.
Then this girl stood up.

> She couldn't have been more than sixteen.
> What if we just stop killing people

no matter our reasons?
Mathematics and literature are antagonistic cultures.
The camera moves steadily on the dolly.
Tempered to break into rounded grains instead of jagged shards.
I orbited the earth forty-eight times aboard *Vostok 6*.
A term for dreamless sleep no longer in scientific use.
What about the love, she asked,

> the love, the love
> the love?

People were laughing and booing.
The studio manager was waving his arms.
The candidate said something about the road to hell.
Updates are ready to install.
Splash paint to achieve a spontaneous effect.
Children gain pleasure from both passing and withholding.
Oyez, oyez, oyez.

> They slipped the surly bonds of earth and touched the face of God.
> Is this thing on?

MEAN FREE PATH

DEDICATION

For the distances collapsed.
      For the figure
failed to humanize
the scale. For the work,
the work did nothing but invite us
to relate it to
      the wall.
For I was a shopper in a dark
      aisle.

For the mode of address
      equal to the war
was silence, but we went on
celebrating doubleness.
For the city was polluted
with light, and the world,
      warming.
For I was a fraud
      in a field of poppies.

For the rain made little
      affective adjustments
to the architecture.
For the architecture was a long
lecture lost on me, negative
mnemonics reflecting
      weather
and reflecting
      reflecting.

For I felt nothing,
        which was cool,
totally cool with me.
For my blood was cola.
For my authority was small
involuntary muscles
        in my face.
For I had had some work done
        on my face.

For I was afraid
        to turn
left at intersections.
For I was in a turning lane.
For I was signaling,
despite myself,
        the will to change.
For I could not throw my voice
        away.

For I had overslept,
        for I had dressed
in layers for the long
dream ahead, the recurring
dream of waking with
alternate endings
        she'd walk me through.
For Ariana.

        For Ari.

MEAN FREE PATH

I finished the reading and looked up
Changed in the familiar ways. Now for a quiet place
To begin the forgetting. The little delays
Between sensations, the audible absence of rain
Take the place of objects. I have some questions
But they can wait. Waiting is the answer
I was looking for. Any subject will do
So long as it recedes. Hearing the echo
Of your own blood in the shell but picturing
The ocean is what I meant by

§

You startled me. I thought you were sleeping
In the traditional sense. I like looking
At anything under glass, especially
Glass. *You* called *me.* Like overheard
Dreams. I'm writing this one as a woman
Comfortable with failure. I promise I will never
But the predicate withered. If you are
Uncomfortable seeing this as portraiture
Close your eyes. No, *you* startled

Identical cities. How sad. Buy up the run
The unsigned copies are more valuable
I have read your essay about the new
Closure. My favorite parts I cannot follow
Surface effects. We moved to Canada
Without our knowledge. If it reciprocates the gaze
How is it pornography? Definitions crossed
With stars, the old closure, which reminds me
Wave to the cameras from the

§

The petals are glass. That's all you need to know
Lines have been cut and replaced
With their opposites. Did I say that out loud
A beautiful question. Barbara is dead
Until I was seventeen, I thought windmills
Turned from the fireworks to watch
Their reflection in the tower
Made wind. Brushed metal apples
Green to the touch

All pleads for an astounding irrelevance
Structured like a language, but I
I like the old music, the audible kind
We made love to in the crawl space
Without our knowledge. Robert is dead
Take my voice. I don't need it. Take my face
I have others. Pathos whistles through the typos
Parentheses slam shut. I'm writing this one
With my eyes closed, listening to the absence of

§

Surface effects. Patterns of disappearance. I
I kind of lost it back there in the trees, screaming
About the complexity of intention, but
But nothing. Come to bed. Reference is a woman
Comfortable with failure. The surface is dead
Wave to the cameras from the towers
Built to sway. I promised I would never
Tell me, whose hand is this. A beautiful
Question her sources again

Unhinged in a manner of speaking
Crossed with stars, a rain that can be paused
So we know we're dreaming on our feet
Like horses in the city. How sad. Maybe
No maybes. Take a position. Don't call it
Night-vision green. Think of the children
Running with scissors through the long
Where were we? If seeing this as portraiture
Makes you uncomfortable, wake up

§

Wake up, it's time to begin
The forgetting. Direct modal statements
Wither under glass. A little book for Ari
Built to sway. I admire the use of felt
Theory, like swimming in a storm, but object
To antirepresentational bias in an era of
You're not listening. I'm sorry. I was thinking
How the beauty of your singing reinscribes
The hope whose death it announces. Wave

In an unconscious effort to unify my voice
I swallow gum. An old man weeps in the airport
Over a missed connection. The color of money is
Night-vision green. Ari removes the bobby pins
I remove the punctuation. Our freezer is empty
Save for vodka and film. Leave the beautiful
Questions unanswered. There are six pages left
Of our youth and I would rather swallow my tongue
Than waste them on description

§

A cry goes up for plain language
In identical cities. Zukofsky appears in my dreams
Selling knives. Each exhibit is a failed futurity
A star survived by its own light. Glass anthers
Confuse bees. Is that pornography? Yes, but
But nothing. Come to reference. A mode of undress
Equal to fascism becomes obligatory
In identical cities. Did I say that already? Did I say
The stranglehold of perspective must be shaken off

A live tradition broadcast with a little delay
Takes the place of experience, like portraits
Reciprocating gazes. Zukofsky appears in my dreams
Offering his face. Each of us must ask herself
Why am I clapping? The content is announced
Through disappearance, like fireworks. Wave
After wave of information breaks over us
Without our knowledge. If I give you my denim
Will you simulate distress

§

To lay everything waste in the name of renewal
Haven't we tried that before? Yes, but
But not in Canada. The vanguard succumbs
To a sense of its own importance as easily as swans
Succumb to the flu. I'm writing this one
With my nondominant hand in the crawl space
Under the war. I can feel an axis snapping
In my skull, and soon I will lose the power
To select, while retaining the power to

All these flowers look the same to me
Night-vision green. There is nothing to do
In the desert but read *Penthouse* and lift weights
My blood is negative. That's all you need to know
Sophisticated weaponry marries the traditional
Pleasures of perspective to the new materiality
Of point-and-click. I'm writing this one
As a woman comfortable with leading
A prisoner on a leash

§

Combine was the word I was looking for
Back there in the trees. My blood is
Scandinavian Modern. I kind of lost it
But enough about me. To return with a difference
Haven't we tried that before? Yes, but
But not from the air. Unique flakes form
Indistinguishable drifts in a process we call
All these words look the same to me
Fascism. Arrange the flowers by their price

Then, where despair had been, the voice
Of Nina Simone. Parentheses open
On a new gender crossed with stars
Ari removes the bobby pins. Night falls
There is no such thing as non sequitur
When you're in love. Let those who object
To the pathos swallow their tongues. My numb
Rebarbative people, put down your Glocks
And your Big Gulps. We have birthmarks to earn

§

Around 1945 the question becomes: Sleepyhead
Since the world is ending, may I eat the candy
Necklace off your body? Turn the record over
Turn the pillow over. It has a cooler side
Like a vein on the wing of a locust
The seam of hope disclosed by her voice
It cannot save us. But it can remind us
Survival is a butcher's goal. All hands
To the pathos. Let the credits

Bend the plastic stick and break the interior tube
The reaction emits light, but not heat
The tragedy of dialectics. Sand-sized particles
Of revolutionary possibility fall constantly
Without our knowledge. The capitol lawns
Sparkle with poison. Since the world is ending
Why not let the children touch the paintings
The voice of Nina Simone contains its own
Negation, like a pearl

§

As brand names drift toward the generic
We drift toward fascism, a life in common
Replaced with its image. The predicates
Are glass. I blew them. I'm sorry, sorrier
Than I can say on such a tiny phone. You're
Breaking up. No, down. I held the hand
Of a complete stranger during takeoff
Unaware it was my own, laying bare
The ideological function of

Numbness, felt silence, a sudden
Inability to swallow, the dream in which
The face is Velcro, describing the film
In the language of disaster, the disaster in
Not finishing sentences, removing the suicide
From the speed dial, failing to recognize
Yourself in the photo, coming home to find
A circle of concerned family and friends
It's more of an artists' colony than a hospital

§

It's more of a vitamin than an antipsychotic
Collective despair expressed in I-statements
The dream in which the skin is stonewashed
Denim, running your hand through the hair
Of an imaginary friend, rising from bed
Dressing, returning calls, all without
Waking, the sudden suspicion the teeth
In your mouth are not your own, let
Alone the words

She handed me a book. I had read it before
Dismissed it, but now, in the dark, I heard
The little delays. If you would speak of love
Stutter, like rain, like Robert, be
Be unashamed. Let those who object to the
But that's familiar rage. It isn't a system
It is a gesture whose power derives from its
Failure, a child attempting to gather
Us into her glitter-flecked arms

§

It isn't a culture of fear. When a people
Pats itself on the back with a numb hand
It isn't a culture at all. Take a position
Cut it off. Leave the rings. The president
But you promised you wouldn't mention
I saw myself in the mirrored lenses
You cannot kill a metonym
Of his bodyguards. I'm moving to Canada
When I wake up. You mean *if*

No concept of clockwise rotation can be
Described on the surface continuously
So this might take a while. Bring a book
Have you tried breaking it into triangles
Or changing hands. No, handedness
Fascia, a tangent bundle. Can we unfold
What we can't figure? Not without making
Cuts. Orient me, for the night is coming
Amphichiral, manifold, and looped

§

We have no reason to hope, but what's reason
What's reason got to do with it? Accent
Not duration. Cantillation, not punctuation
And that's love. Why not speak of it
As we are drawn up into the rising
Toroidal fireball? This column
Of powdery light is made possible
By Boeing, but what, and here's where people
Start disappearing, made Boeing possible

If you could see the tip of the vector
It would appear to be moving in a circle
As it approached you. Reference is a slow
Wave transporting energy through empty
Media. You can't rush it. The displaced
Pathos returns with a vengeance and painters
Pull grids apart in grief. Only a master
Only a butcher can unmake sense. The rest of us
Have axes to grind into glass

§

By *complex* I mean my intention is drawn
Downward to the bottom of the cloud
It hurts me when you listen too closely
Smothering reference. Carefully decanted
Left to breathe. *That's* criticism. The subject
Rises to the surface. Bursts. All light paths
From the object to the image are reversible
And that hurts, to know it didn't have to be
I mean, don't get me wrong, I enjoy killing

Birds were these little ships that flew and sang
There are some cool pics online. Funny
Strange, not ha-ha funny, how the black
Canvas grows realistic, a bird's-eye view
Of their disappearance. Wave after wave
Of déjà lu. After the storm, the sky turns
Night-vision green. The color of murder
I can hear the soldiers marching in my
Pillow. Even in Canada

§

Her literature is irrelevant to October
Anna of all the Russias, whose body was
An ideal October that has yet to obtain
A face. October approached asymptotically
By tanks. The leaves turn night-vision
Anna, do you see how the sand-sized particles
Of the true October rise from the asphalt
Like fireflies whose bodies are night-vision
Neither do I. The irrelevant I. The I of all

It will develop recursively or not at all
The new closure. In lieu of fixed outlines
Modulating color. If concentrated light
Strikes the leaf, part is reflected through
The droplet, producing a white glow around
The genre. It's like the whispering gallery
The fighter pilot sees his shadow on the cloud
Crossed with the Wailing Wall. We can't
Distinguish rounds of ammunition from

§

Applause. Speak plainly. Keep your hands
On the table. Do not flee into procedure
Do not wait for a surpassing disaster
To look your brother in the eye and speak
Of love. Make no mistake: the disjunction
The disjunction stays. Do not hesitate
To cut the most beautiful line in the name
Of form. The bread of words. Look for me
At genre's edge. I'm going there on foot

I dyed what's-her-face's hair with lime
Kool-Aid so when I read "Bezhin Meadow"
I lent her aspect to the green-haired spirit
There is a girl trapped in every manmade lake
She will pull you into your reflection
Stephen tells me what's-her-face
Who used to sleepwalk into the snow
Piss her name and glide back to bed
Without waking was thrown

§

Into this poem through a windshield
Once she gathered me into her glitter-flecked
I don't care if "aspect" is archaic
Once she walked into the sliding door
A plane announced through disappearance
You made it this far without mentioning
Topeka. Glass in her hair. Patterns of
I will throw my voice like a clay pot
Keep her ashes there. I don't care if "love

I don't deny the influence, but it's less
A relation of father to son than a relation of
Moon to tide. Plus, my teachers are mainly
Particles bombarding gold foil or driving rain
It's the motion, not the material, not the nouns
But the little delays. A gender crossed
A genre crossed on foot by Marvin Gaye
Filicide. Strong misreadings arise
On the surface. Burst. It didn't have to be

§

If I rise from table, if I wander
Discalced through the sparkling lawns
If I'm lost in Juárez in Topeka, if it's winter
In August when the prodromata, when the birds
Cite the past in all its moments, there is no
No need for examples, police, doctors
Let me walk to the edge of the genre and look out
Into nothing. I will return, the fit will return me
In time for coffee and oranges

Authority derived from giving it away
Is how I define *aura,* like Zukofsky's
Paper flowers picked from *Kapital*
For Celia's hair. Priceless. The high
Reflective ceilings allow us to receive
Our own applause. When an audience
Takes a bow, that's fascism. A looped
Encore. Surface effects. The auditorium
Is a standing wave. A sedimented roar

§

The entire system weighs about two pounds
A small bird governs the atria. You dream
The donor's dreams. The donor's breath
Breaks your lines across their prepositions
Halved and polished to display the crystal
Back-formations. Go in fear of abstraction
But go. Be gone by morning. There is nothing
You don't need a shell. Just cup your hand
Nothing for you here but repetition

DOPPLER ELEGIES

§

By any measure, it was endless
        winter. Emulsions with
Then circled the lake like
This is it. This April will be
Inadequate sensitivity to green. I rose
early, erased for an hour
        Silk-brush and ax
I'd like to think I'm a different person
        latent image fading

around the edges and ears
        Overall a tighter face
now. Is it so hard for you to understand
From the drop-down menu
In a cluster of eight poems, I selected
sleep, but could not
        I decided to change everything
Composed entirely of stills
        or fade into the trees

but could not
        remember the dream
save for one brief shot
of a woman opening her eyes
Ari, pick up. I'm a different person
In a perfect world, this would be
        April, or an associated concept
Green to the touch
        several feet away

§

I want to finish the book in time
       period. Confused bees
In a perfect world
a willow-effect. Rain on the recording
Fine with this particular form
of late everything, a spherical
       break of colored stars
a voice described as torn in places
       Why am I always

asleep in your poems
       Soft static falling through
The life we've chosen
from a drop-down menu
of available drives. Look at me
Ben, when am I
       This isn't my voice
At such-and-such smooth rate, the lines
       Stream at night

and love. Why not speak of it
       as all work now
is late work. Leafage, fountain, cloud
into whose sunlit depths
I'm quoting. Is there a place for this
she cut her hair
       She held it toward me
In your long dream
       money changes hands

§

I'm worried about a friend
        among panicles of spent
flowers. I'm on the phone
There's an argument here regarding
Cathedral windows thicker at the base
It does not concern you
        flowing glass. Can we talk
about the drinking
        They call them smoke trees

I'm pretty much dead
        by any measure
already. When we were kids, the leaves
but that's a story, fallen or reflected
obscured the well. I cut this
In the dream, they are always
        younger. Ari woke me
You were screaming
        Everything is so

easy for you
        You mean was
so easy, like walking slowly
Out of the photo, even those
They are blooming early. I mean that
literally. You can see it from space
        he took. Can we talk
about the drinking
        Sometime in May

§

The passengers are asked to clap
       It was always the same
window in his poems
for the two soldiers. We were delayed
In every seat, a tiny screen
A tiny bottle. The same traffic
       High up in the trees, small
rain. He held the subject
       constant. Now I

get it. I looked out
       over Denver, but could see
only our reflection. Dim
the cabin lights. Robert is dead
Articles may have shifted
I didn't know him. Why am I
       clapping. We are beginning
our final descent into
       A voice described as torn

On the recording, I could hear
       the hesitation
A certain courage. I can't explain
as music. We could watch
our own plane crash. We would be
Our men and women
       permitted to call down
in uniform. When I heard him live
       it was lost on me

§

A flowering no one attends
   The enterprise known
variously as waking, April, or
Bats are disappearing like
color into function. I wanted to open
In a new window
   the eyes of a friend
by force if necessary. Amber light
   is a useless phrase

but will have to do
   what painting did
Dense smoke from the burning wells
for our parents. Ben
there is a man at the door who says
I've made small changes
   he found your notebook
throughout in red. The recurring dream
   contrived in places

Of waning significance
   it resembles the hand
after a difficult passage
opening, a key word in the early
Blue of rippled glass
atonal circles. They phased us out
   across the backward capitals
like paper money
   Or is that two words

§

They are passing quickly, those
        houses I wanted to
speak in. Empty sets
Among my friends, there is a fight about
The important questions
cannot arise, so those must be hills
        where the famous
winter. I am familiar with the dream
        Windmills enlarge

experience, killing birds
        but I have already used
dream too often in my book
of relevance. Nothing can be predicated
Along the vanishing coast
tonight. You'll have to wait until
        remnants of small fires
the eye can pull new features from
        The stars

eat here. There is a private room
        Are you concerned
about foreign energy
In your work, I sense a certain
distance, like a radio left on
Across the water, you can see
        the new construction going up
is glass. The electric cars
        unmanned

§

Somewhere in this book I broke
  There is a passage
with a friend. I regret it now
lifted verbatim from
Then began again, my focus on
moving the lips, failures in
  The fuselage glows red against
rinsed skies. Rehearsing sleep
  I think of him from time

in a competitive field
  facedown, a familiar scene
composed entirely of stills
to time. It's hard to believe
When he calls, I pretend
he's gone. He was letting himself go
  I'm on the other line
in a cluster of eight poems
  all winter. The tenses disagreed

for Ari. Sorry if I've seemed
  distant, it's been a difficult
period, striking as many keys
with the flat of the hand
as possible, then leaning the head
against the window, unable to recall
  April, like overheard speech
at the time of writing
  soaked into its length

§

Is this what you meant by prose
        Silica glass shapes
A supporting beam
where lightning strikes the sand
missing from the voice, eaten away
From the inside I could see
        his influence, mainly in the use
but also in exchange
        The head tipped back

to slow the speaking
        Our collaboration ends
On the appointed day, we gathered
in a makeshift structure
Viscous fluid from a floral source
but quarreled over terms
        pouring from the mouth into
Particles of wax. It's been done before
        cupped hands

in a lesser key, a broader sense
        I sound like him
more often now, unable to pronounce
or trailing off, then suddenly
Set against a large expanse
I have to leave. I just remembered
        something about Ari
structured like a language
        with appropriate delays

MEAN FREE PATH

What if I made you hear this as music
But not how you mean that. The slow beam
Opened me up. Walls walked through me
Like resonant waves. I thought that maybe
If you aren't too busy, we could spend our lives
Parting in stations, promising to write
War and Peace, this time with feeling
As bullets leave their luminous traces across
Wait, I wasn't finished. I was going to say
Breakwaters echo long lines of cloud

§

Renunciation scales. Exhibits shade
Imperceptibly into gift shops. The death of a friend
Opens me up. Suddenly the weather
Is written by Tolstoy, whose hands were giant
Resonant waves. It's hard not to take
When your eye is at the vertex of a cone
Autumn personally. My past becomes
Of lines extending to each leaf
Citable in all its moments: parting, rain

There must be an easier way to do this
I mean without writing, without echoes
Arising from focusing surfaces, which should
Should have been broken by structures
Hung from the apex in the hope of deflecting
In the hope of hearing the deflection of music
As music. There must be a way to speak
At a canted angle of enabling failures
The little collisions, the path of decay

§

But before it was used by the blind, it was used
By soldiers who couldn't light their lamps
Without drawing fire from across the lake
Embossed symbols enable us to read
Our orders silently in total dark
In total war, the front is continuous
Night writing, from which descends
Night-vision green. What if I made you
Hear this with your hands

Autumn in a minor novel. The school
Scatters, scattering light across the surface
Re-forms around the ankle of the child
That you were. The end. Put the book away
Look out the window: we are descending
Like Chopin through the dusk. Now it's six
Six years later and I'm reading it again
Over Denver. I bought it in the gift shop
Nothing's changed except the key

§

Little contrasts flicker in
Distances complex because collapsing
Under their own weight like stars
Embossed symbols. I can't compete
It's like the moment after waking
When you cannot determine if the screaming
With devices designed to amplify
Was internal or external to the dream
Starlight so soldiers can read in their sleep

Wait, I don't want this to turn
Turn into a major novel. I want this to be
Composed entirely of edges, a little path
For Ari. All my teachers have been women
But not how you mean that. That's why I speak
In a voice so soft it sounds like writing
Night writing. A structure of feeling
Broken by hand. I want the paper to have poor
Opacity, the verso just visible beneath

§

The ode just visible beneath the elegy
The preemptive elegy composed entirely
This movement from the ground to cloud
Of waves decaying slowly on plucked strings
Is lightning. I don't know how else to say it
I mean without writing. Maybe if you let
The false starts stand, stand in for symbols
Near collapse, or let collapsing symbolize
The little clearing loving is. Maybe then

Stamp the interference pattern into green foil
Tear the hologram in half. You still see
The whole landscape, only lower resolution
Only through rain. They call this redundancy
In the literature. It has to do with reference beams
Lines extending to each leaf. As I turned the
They call this contingency, a kind of music
Page I tore it, and now it's elegy
It's autumn. Foils are starting to fall

§

There are three hundred sixty-two thousand
And that's love. There are flecks of hope
Eight hundred eighty ways to read each stanza
Deep in traditional forms like flaws
Visible when held against the light
I did not walk here all the way from prose
To make corrections in red pencil
I came here tonight to open you up
To interference heard as music

Damaged by flashes, the canvas begins
To enlist the participation of the viewer
To resemble the sitter. Looming sheets
Work mirror flake into the surface
Of curved steel create spaces we can't enter
In that sense is it public sculpture
Beside the office park reflecting pool
I panic my little panic. The death of a
The caesura scales. Autumn tapers

§

Waking in stations, writing through rain
Which, when it first mixes with exhaust
Smells like jasmine. These are the little
Floating signatures that interest me
Collisions along the path of reference
This time with feeling. What I cannot say is
Is at the vertex. Build your own predicates
In a hand so faint it reads like parting
Out of shifting constellations of debris

I decided to work against my fluency
I was tired of my voice, how it stressed
Its quality as object with transparent darks
This is a recording. This living hand
Reached in error. I hold it toward you
Throw it toward you, measuring the time
Before the waves return from paper walls
Across the lake. Hang up and try again
With poor opacity, with feeling

§

I decided I would come right out and say it
Into a hollow enclosure producing the
The aural illusion that we are in a canyon
They call this an experience of structure
Or a cave. If it weren't for Ari
In the literature. It has to do with predicates
But it is. I had planned a work of total outrage
Changing phase upon reflection
Until a wave of jasmine interfered

The bird is a little machine for forgetting
The freight trains that pass my house
Every fifteen minutes do not cause any object
In the house to shake except my body
Which makes it seem as if every object
In my house is shaking violently
Is my answer to your question regarding
Content. A better way to put this is
The bird is a little machine

§

For total war, the memory of jasmine
Paired organs allow us to experience
Contradiction without contradiction
Flowering in winter. Is my answer audible
Or mine, whatever it might mean
Relative to scattering, or am I quoting
The formant frequencies of anchors
What I cannot say. I stand for everything
Like money changing hands in dreams

In the literature. What if I made you
Music that resembles twigs or mimics
Read this as the evolutionary pressure
The meandering lines of the mottled pattern
Obliterate the contours of the soldier
The behavior of a leaf in wind, a feather
To disappear into my surroundings slowly
Infrared is emitted, not reflected. The bodies
Vanish as they cool. They call this crypsis

§

An elaborate allegorization is taking place
In a hollow enclosure as we speak
The question is how to reconcile sleep
An unexpected movement near the face
Cycles with visiting hours. Nocturnal species
Startles me. I nearly wake before regrouping
Yoked together by a common implied verb
To form a flying wedge. Look out
The symbols are collapsing

I'm not above being understood, provided
The periodic motion takes the form of
Work is done on the surface to disturb
Traveling waves. The distances increase
The manmade lake. Metals that behave
In value as the last observer turns away
Like water give us courage to dissolve
And walks out of the frame into
The genre, but not the strength. Wait

§

I wasn't finished. I was going to say
Into the open, a green place when seen
Through goggles. Virgil wrote at night
From above. Build your own pastoral
Out of embossed symbols, hollow enclosures
Expand on impact in order to disrupt
The Lady of the Lake. A magazine for men
More tissue as they travel through
The genre. We were happy in the cave

I planned a work that could describe itself
Into existence, then back out again
Until description yielded to experience
Yielded an experience of structure
Collapsing under its own weight like
Citable in all its moments: parting
Dusk. Look out the window. Those small
Rain. In a holding pattern over Denver
Collisions clear a path from ground to cloud

§

Across the lake. I thought that maybe
If there aren't wolves to ring our settlement
It's public sculpture in the sense that
Like everybody else in the gift shop
A refrigerator magnet. Two big bags
I wanted to see what the soldier bought
We could invent some wilderness
Before returning to his dystopic errand
Of mirror flake. A magazine for men

The leaves appear to increase in brightness
The dim star in the periphery disappears
At dusk as rods shift toward the shorter waves
If you turn and try to look at it directly
It maps onto the fovea, rich in cones
Which privilege color over line. I turned
I tore it. Now I see the elegy beneath
Long lines of cloud with poor opacity
A pattern stamped into green foil

§

With feeling, how the eye moves constantly
To keep light from the object falling
Gently on a little clearing. They call this
Like rain that never reaches ground
Reading, like birds that lure predators away
Virga, or the failure of the gaze to reach
By faking injury, like flares that bend
Across the lake in total dark
Missiles from their path

The good news is light is scattered such
Toxicity means the paint must be applied
The apparent brightness of the surface
By robots one atom at a time, bad news
Is the same regardless of the angle of view
I thought I should be the one to tell you
Simultaneously, how monks sing chords
A kind of silence, what we might call
The military applications of Cézanne

§

Its physics occurred to me while falling
Through rain that wasn't moving. I woke
Before I reached the ground like virga
To find Ari gone. The flattened stems
Only because there was no ground
Allow the words to tremble in the breath
As such. There is no way to read this
Once, and that's love, or aloud, and that's
Breakwaters echo long lines of cloud

Luciferin oxidized by luciferase: night
Writing. They begin to synchronize
Vision green. These are the little floating
Their flashing at the approach of mates
Signatures. Now it is all coming back to me
Or prey. No, I project the false totality
From across the lake in the form of smooth
Reverberant decay. I don't see color
Without tearing off their wings

§

Is why I'm comfortable with her dream
If you find it maudlin, cut and paste
Of a world without men, but not how you
Is why I cannot touch her with the hand
And another thing: breakwaters echo
A false totality. The goal is to fail
Synchronically, until description yields
Interference rippling across faces
And another thing: the seas

The pitch drops suddenly because the source
Passed away last night in Brooklyn
Hanged himself from the apex in the hope
Left a rent check, a letter in a hand
So faint it read like falling, evening
Of never reaching ground. The siren
The source has stressed his quality as object
Walks through me, opening me up
Recedes. A rain check. This isn't music

§

Sheets of rain create a still space in the city
Where he takes closure into his own hands
We can't enter. This is a holding pattern
This is the lethal suspension of a friend
From a low beam by ligature. Noncoincidence
Of senses, how you feel the train before
You hear the fighter once you've seen it pass
You hear it, indicates a moving frame
Laid to rest is literature

The fovea burns off like fog. A window
Breaks over me in waves. Space is soft clay
Children imply with sparklers, and I find
Sufficient sadness there to organize a canvas
Packed so densely with figures it appears
Let alone a life. The seas are rising
Blank. The seas have long since whelmed
Those cities of the future where my readers
Were displaced. You are free to leave

§

But not how you mean that, not without
Arising from focusing surfaces charged
Changed in the familiar ways. Little contrasts
With the task of total re-description
To begin the forgetting, a gentle rippling
Across the manmade lake. I planned a work
With appropriate delays, all signals seem
To issue from one speaker. Wait, I wasn't
Continuous in stations, rain

The end. Objects in the dream are sized
He painted what he saw onto the window
According not to distance, but importance
The leaves are falling because his eyes
Because the lines are broken by the breath
Are blank. Questions of accessibility arise
Is lightning. The particles change direction
At funerals. Water spins the other way
Only when I'm asked to read aloud

§

In a voice so soft it sounds like coughing
Blood into a handkerchief in Russia
The minor novel scales. The weather holds
Forming patterns. I am in Brooklyn
Over Denver, imagining October
Light playing on the body of a friend
Written by Tolstoy. Does that make sense
Or should I describe it with my hands
It's hard not to take the music personally

I know it's full of flowers, music, stars, but
But the pressures under which it fails
How it falls apart if read aloud, or falls
What we might call its physics
Together like applause, a false totality
Scales. The words are just there to confuse
The censors, like mock eyes on the wing
Except for *Ari*. No energy is lost if they collide
The censors inside me, and that's love

§

And that's elegy. I know I am a felt
This is the form where my friend is buried
Effect of the things that I take personally
A gentle rippling across the social body
I know that I can't touch her with the hand
That has touched money, I mean without
Several competing forms of closure
Irony, now warm and capable of
Decay on strings as we descend

DOPPLER ELEGIES

§

I want to give you, however
          brief, a sense of
period, a major advancement in
I slept through. I want to understand
I want to return to our earlier
I keep a notebook for
          that purpose by
their motion lights, I didn't want
          to wake you, I

sell windows in
          civilian life, I can sleep
anything, the way some people
here, in the terminal
Even as a child, I could sell
look at me, as if to say, what is he
          sleeping, what is Ben
sleeping now. It is as good a word
          as any

war between the forces of
          I wrote this
quickly, over many years
You may have seen me writing it
In photographs, I never know
what they want me to do
          with my hands, I just
smile, but it doesn't mean
          Orange

§

jumpsuits, they have changed
           painting, I
behind the concertina wire
can't look at it anymore, that wall
across which shadows play
Sorry to be vague
           at such an hour. Were you
When I called, I heard
           my voice

anywhere near waking
           in the background
Strange, reversible lines, I thought
he was dead. He is
better of it, pushing the glass
away. How many songs
           can it hold, that thing
I've seen in windows, has it changed
           singing, or

hooded figures
           I didn't know
it had a camera, some features are
The blue of links, obscure
beneath the face, the green
We still don't have a word for
           Simulated drowning in
embedded streams
           a perfect world

§

warming, we can enter
       our address, they rotate
slowly overhead, the satellites
I imply their passing when
you're reading, do you think
I wanted it to end
       in complicated paths
like minor planets, flowering trees
       or villages

aflame, please find
       your seat, pretend
to be asleep, then am, head against
the shade, or writing in
a minute hand, yellow masks, unless
Small children traveling alone
       there is a screen
or soldiers, so many dots per inch
       The uniform

becomes you
       Seen from space
it hasn't happened yet, the states
I'm quoting from at night
are red. If they assign storms
proper names, why can't I
       Describe the structure of
feel anything, I mean without
       visuals

§

built to sway, the saying goes
        Those stars are where
I made some cuts
The last time I saw him was
more or less at random, long
stretches of implied
        flatness, I can't read my own
innumerable tiny marks
        A rustling of tenses

like distant traffic
        overhead, green
zones. On Election Day, make sure
you think of him here
Between commercials, little
glitches occur, so we know it's live
        around the edges, I
organized, distributed fliers like
        This one

goes out to all
        My people were
possible worlds, encouraging
signs, estimated crowds along
the vanishing coast, tonight
is brought to you
        was brought to me
Unfinished, popular songs
        I gathered

§

quickly, over many years
            Forces are withdrawn
bundled and resold, the words
I distanced myself from
conventional forms, but now
Who am I to say
            at the midpoint of dissolve
I'm sorry, I wasn't listening
            in prose

the weather broke
            When they called
Against the glass, it writes itself
Illuminated prompts
make ordering easy, the way
It's supposed to be a picture of
            flying east, we lost a day
Blank verse returned
            in his later work

To untrained eyes
            it looks like me
Dispersed across regimes, the costs
expressed in human terms
Your machine picked up
the little delays, my intention was
            Occasional
music from a passing car
            for Ari

§

I'd begin again, this time with
            best practices
Inside the ear, small white buds
At odds with all ideas
of scale, last light glinting off
the wing seen from the ground
            A delicate passage
in a so-so film, from dark to darks
            The real

issue here, in the terminal
            I've come to understand
April can be made into
a thing. I guess that's obvious now
When every surface is
a counter, it's hard to eat
            Among my friends
those paintings double as
            the end

of painting, so this might be
            conceptual
For a while, I thought it was
tentatively titled, a reference to
how waves return
In a cluster of eight poems
            until you let go of the keys
damage is sustained
            Applause

§

at each mention of his name
          In the long dream
I left it out, that way
We can have the theater to ourselves
across which shadows play
The voice, because it is recorded
          reminds me of
a slow remorse I sampled from
          Yesterday

they were acting strange
          Now they're almost gone
or symbols, which is worse
After the last hive has collapsed
flowers will be poems
Composed entirely of stills
          it doesn't star
anyone you'd know, believe me
          When I say

love, I mean
          and that's rare
enough, low beams exposed
Our permanent achievement
Unbeknownst to us, obscure
forces are at work
          like a radio left on
On the outskirts of
          identical cities

§

the new construction going up
             is elegy, no
money down or interest through
The twilight of the medium
We're heavily indebted to
interior scenes, now destroyed
             It says so here
On the computer, you can watch
             The seas

are rising, but
             But nothing
anywhere near waking
In the crawl space, we prepared
brief, discontinuous remarks
designed to fall apart
             When read aloud
it reminds me of that time we saw
             silent films

accompanied by
             Her breathing was
a rustling of tenses, underground
Movements have become
citable in all their moments
With my nondominant hand
             I want to give
in a minor key
             the broadest sense

THE DARK THREW PATCHES
DOWN UPON ME ALSO

It was not my intention to travel in time,
watch him distribute dried fruit and sweet
crackers to soldiers in hospital, small sums,
writing their letters, this was back when
you might take it to a cousin to be read
under a cut glass lamp. Why do articles fall out
over time, or get put back in, is that a good
question for the poet if I meet him abroad, aboard
one of several no longer extant ferries?
I am an alien here with a residency, light
alien to me, true hawks starting from the trees
at my footfall on gravel, sun-burnt from reading
Specimen Days on the small porch across
the street from where another poet died
or began dying. Some residents request it,
others request not to be assigned it, I
made no requests, but still end up traveling
by tram across wartime Manhattan when
the bridge was probably the tallest structure.
No, it wouldn't be completed until, wouldn't
have been completed yet, those are still
my favorite tenses, moths around streetlights
obscuring the casualty lists I'm trying to read
aloud to citizens in formal dress, address,
attempting to stay cool and extant.
I don't make any sense in the high desert,
grip the yellow can with a toothed wheel,
find, instead of coffee, ash, particulate, but
brew it and walk over with a cup for him.
Wake and reread the section about gifts:
it might be worse to love both sides in a war,
a general engagement in the woods, to speak
of a wound's "neighborhood" as they remove

splinters of bone, worse to admire singing
through candlelit gauze than to ignore
a wedding party struck by unmanned drones:
I know no one involved except everyone,
let alone love. They are dead in different ways,
these poets, but I visit them both because
a residency affords me time, not sure where
the money comes from, or what money is,
how you could set it beside a soldier's bed
then walk out across the moonlit mall in love
with the federal, wake up refreshed and bring
tobacco to those who haven't received
wounds in the lung or the face. Tonight
I listen to their recordings at once
in separate windows, four lines from "America"
might be recited by an actor, but the noise
of the wax cylinder is real, sounds how I
imagine engines of old boats would, while
"The Door" incorporates distress into the voice,
could be in the room. The former says
he waits for me ahead, but I doubt I'll arrive
in time: even the phrase "evening papers"
will need a gloss, like the notion presidents
have features. Instead I project myself back
before carbon arc and mercury vapor, invisible
labor of men in the dimly lit caissons
still a few years in the future, when the danger
will be coming up too fast, nitrogen
bubbles forming in the blood. I wanted to say
I also pass through a series of airlocks en route
to imperceptible work, even that a tower of a sort
might be built upon it, but I'm more a supervisor
ill from surfacing quickly, watching its progress

through a telescope, sending messages to
the bridge-site through my good wife, Emily.
When completed, the celebration will surpass
the one that marked the closing of the war, as if
you could separate those things, as if those were
things, cheap oak and iron deployed
as inflation rages. My father studied briefly
with Hegel, and there are other proper names
we could summon: both Cranes, the one
who lived in this apartment, drowned
himself at my age, and the older one who died
younger, having both seen and not seen war.
But that's just the game of features again,
when in fact the unwounded face is smooth.

A thin crescent hangs over a Brooklyn where
the rich still farm and I wait for your return
from a war you love all sides of: come back
to the future where I'm resident and the phrase
evokes one of the crucial movies of my youth
set in 1955, the year nuclear power first
lit up a town: Arco, Idaho, also home to the first
meltdown (1961), although years are part
of the game. In the movie they lack plutonium
to power the time-traveling car, whereas
in real life it seeps into the Fukushima soil,
Back to the Future was ahead of its time,
1985, when I was six and the Royals took
the series, in part because a ridiculous call
forced game seven, Orta clearly out at first
in replays. I can feel it getting away from me
so I leave the house, use the back door to avoid
the other residents, and watch the sun

set through smoke from Arizona fires, "zero
percent contained," wave to a woman bent
over a row of yellow flowers, but she can't
see me: I've faded from the photograph.
We often say twilight but mean dusk,
or check our watches without noting the time,
two of the minor practices that make us
enough of a people to believe that a raid
on the compound can bring closure. Depends
what you think is ending, the gentle face
of terror, civilian nuclear power, are those
two things? There are men at work on the roof
when I return, too hot to do by day, wave
and am seen, an awkward exchange
in Spanish, who knows what I said, having
confused the conditional with imperfect.
Norteño from their radio fills the house
I hope they know isn't mine: I just write here.
Walk back out with a Brita and three glasses,
but of course they have their own water, can
I offer you a cup of ashes, can I interest you?
Soon they move on to the house I call his
because Douglas, who manages the compound,
rushed him from there to hospital in Midland
or Odessa, the roofers' purpose obscure to me,
whose work is to chat with the dying or dead,
to let them lay a pale hand on my knee
if they still have hands, the practical nurses
busy behind curtains, some of them singing
popular hymns, often accompanied on melodeon,
an accordion or small organ, strange
to have either available among the cots
and mosquito netting. It seems to be pleasurable

for him when the moon makes radiant patches
for a death-stricken boy to moan in, or
a patch of the wood ignites, consuming
soldiers too crippled to flee. "Patch" from
the Latin, *pedaeum*, literally something
measured, compare to the Medieval *pedāre*:
to measure in feet. That might be false,
the point is he feels no need to contain his love
for the material richness of their dying, federal
body from which extremities secede, a pail
beside the bed for that purpose, almost never
mentions race, save to note there are plenty
of black soldiers, clean black women would
make wonderful nurses, while again and again
I deliver money to boys with perforated organs:
"unionism," to die with shining hair
beside fractional currency, part of writing
the greatest poem. Or is the utopian moment
loving the smell of shit and blood, brandy
as it trickles through the wound, politics of pure
sensation? When you die in the patent-office
there's a pun on expiration, you must enter one
of the immense glass cases filled with scale
models of machines, utensils, curios. Look,
your president will be shot in a theater,
actors will be presidents, the small sums
will grow monstrous as they circulate, measure:
I have come from the future to warn you.

Tomorrow I'll see the Donald Judd
permanent installations in old hangars, but
now it's tomorrow and I didn't go, set out hatless
in the early afternoon, got lost and was soon

seeing floaters and spots, so returned to the house,
the interior sea green until my eyes adjusted,
I lay down for a while and dreamt I saw it.
Tonight I'll shave, have two drinks with a friend
of a friend, but that was last week and I cancelled,
claimed altitude had sickened me a little, can
we get back in touch when I've adjusted?
Yesterday I saw the Donald Judd in a book
they keep in the house, decided not to go until
I finished a poem I've since abandoned
but will eventually pick back up. What I need
is a residency within the residency, then
I could return refreshed to this one, take in Judd
with friends of friends, watch the little spots
of blood bloom on the neck, so I'll know
I've shaved in time, whereas now I'm as close
to a beard as I've been, but not very close.
Shaving is a way to start the workday by ritually
not cutting your throat when you've the chance,
"Washes and razors for foofoos—
for me freckles and a bristling beard,"
a big part of reading him is embarrassment.
Woke up today having been shaved in a dream
by a nurse who looked like Falconetti,
my cot among the giant aluminum boxes
I still plan to see, then actually shaved and felt
that was work enough for one day, my back
to the future. The foundation is closed
Sundays and nights, of which the residency
is exclusively composed, so plan your visit
well in advance, or just circle the building
where the Chamberlain sculptures are housed,
painted and chromium plated-steel, best

viewed through your reflection in the window:
In Bastien-Lepage's *Joan of Arc* (1879)
she reaches her left arm out, maybe for support
in the swoon of being called, but instead
of grasping branches or leaves, her hand,
in what is for me the crucial passage, partially
dissolves. It's carefully positioned
on the diagonal sightline of one of three
hovering, translucent angels he was attacked
for failing to reconcile with the future saint's
realism, a "failure" the hand presents
as a breakdown of space, background
beginning to swallow her fingers, reminding me
of the photograph people fade from, the one
"Marty" uses to measure the time remaining
for the future in which we watched the movie,
only here it's the future's presence, not
absence that eats away at her hand: you can't
rise from the loom so quickly that you
overturn the stool and rush toward the plane
of the picture without startling the painter, hear
voices the medium is powerless to depict
without that registering somewhere on the body.
But from our perspective, it's precisely
where the hand ceases to signify a hand
and is paint, no longer appears to be warm
or capable, that it reaches the material
present, becomes realer than sculpture because
tentative: she is surfacing too quickly.
This is why her face is in my dream, not hers,
but the beautiful actress that played her (1928),
also because in the film she recants her false
confession, achieves transcendence

only after her head is shaved. I'm embarrassed
because there are workers on the roof
for whom this is the north, and no one calls
from beyond the desert frame except a poet
or two, the conflict between two systems
of incompatible labor endures, and the third
is the flickering border between them,
the almost-work of taking everything personally
until the person becomes a commons,
a radical "loafing" that embraces the war
because it also dissolves persons, a book
that aspires to the condition of currency. Warhol
wanted to make a movie of *Specimen Days*.

Some say the glowing spheres near Route 67
are paranormal, others dismiss them as
atmospheric tricks: static, swamp gas, reflections
of headlights and small fires, but why dismiss
what misapprehension can establish, our own
illumination returned to us as alien, as sign?
They've built a concrete viewing platform
lit by low red lights which must appear
mysterious when seen from what it overlooks.
Tonight I see no spheres, but project myself
and then gaze back, an important trick because
the goal is to be on both sides of the poem,
shuttling between the you and I. But what
is the mystery he claims his work both does
and doesn't contain, what does he promise,
say we have silently accepted, cannot state,
and how is it already accomplished as we read,
and who is being addressed in the last stanza
of "Crossing Brooklyn Ferry?" Form

is always the answer to the riddle it poses, though
there isn't much of one here, just a speaker
emptied of history so he can ferry across it:
tide, wake, barge, flag, foundry are things
anyone could see, but no one in particular,
less things than examples of things, which once
meant a public meeting place, assembly.
Words are the promise he can't make
in words without rendering them determinate
and thereby breaking the promise because
only when empty can we imagine assembling,
not as ourselves, but as representatives
of the selves he has asked us to dissolve:
dumb ministers. These are the contradictory
conditions of my residency in the poem,
where Ari isn't allowed to join me because
she's from the world, and what I miss most
is the distortion, noise of the wax cylinder,
the flaws in the medium that preserve
what distance it closes, source of the glow
I return to Creeley for. I wanted to include
her daily reports on how the lavender held up
throughout the heat wave, the dilated root
where my aorta meets my heart, how I mistook
two moths drawn to the flashlight for
the eyeshine of some animal approaching
in the dark, good to know that I can still
feel an almost sexual terror on these meds.
Then I had big plans for stinging ants
as a figure of collectivity experienced
as weird fact of the privileged residency,
wasted a morning baiting them with apple,
blushing hard when Douglas asked. Don't ask:

the place where the intern's shoulder curves
into her breast, the altitude-induced
nosebleed that I slept through, beard of blood
in the bathroom mirror, terrible phrase
stuck in my head for a week, the chances of
distant recurrence somewhere in my mother,
small rain on the skylight, having learned
to distinguish begging calls of baby swallows
from the chatter of adults. A friend in California
believes he is breathing in hot particles
from Fukushima, where a rabbit has been born
without ears, should I include that here
along with the other casualties, or will
everything be leveled as soon as it appears
in the catalog? My favorite part of the book:
he's in Topeka and is supposed to read
a poem to twenty thousand people, instead
decides to write a speech he fails to give
because he's having a great time at dinner,
so he just puts the speech in the book where we
can read it at our leisure, makes you wonder
if he actually sent the letter he included
written to a dead soldier's mother. Whitman:
poetry replaced by oratory addressed
to the future, the sensorial commons
abandoned for a private meal. If only there were
more wandering away from the stage, less
tallying, one of his favorite verbs, I could
turn to him now, but the reflection
of his head is haloed by spokes of light, "cross"
is in the title, and there are other signs
of a negative incarnation, paper heaven
where the suffering is done by others.

I've been worse than unfair, although he was
asking for it, is still asking for it, I can hear
him asking for it through me when I speak,
despite myself, to a people that isn't there,
or think of art as leisure that is work
in houses the undocumented build, repair.
It's among the greatest poems and fails
because it wants to become real and can
only become prose, founding mistake
of the book from which we've been expelled.
And yet: look out from the platform, see
mysterious red lights move across the bridge
in a Brooklyn I may or may not return to,
phenomena no science can explain,
wheeled vehicles rushing through the dark
with their windows down, streaming music.

– Marfa, June 2011

CONTRE-JOUR

The light that changes
the light that goes out
when you pass under it
The unsafe intersection
and the ghost bike
The light that turns out to be a flame
and the bulb designed
to flicker. Obviously
city lights, the necklace
lights of bridges, lights of planes
are part of this, especially
      flashing or
extinguished

      Trick candle
sparking in the cake, little star
sparking, wintergreen
in the mouth, the speech of it
decaying, flash
of the muzzles as they chased
Victor Serge across the rooftops
The snow blue in the light
and the burning manuscripts
and Paris, the city of
the light that changes
      in the mouth
I wish I'd known

      you were a fan of light
I would have saved some for you
Moonlight on pavement set
aside for you, in factories
in prisons, obviously

and Moscow burning obviously
in the throat I left
a light on for you, Victor Serge
in the last century, century of last
cigarettes, the light
decay gives off, the cold
       light of the living
organism

       in the open
seas, in Oakland, some
old paintings. Because like ash
it scatters, I thought that I might sing
Because it dies repeatedly
in Mexico, penniless
Penniless in Spain
I thought that I might speak
openly with you in photographs
If I appear, then obviously
I'm penniless, because appearance is
       the last resort
of light

       Victor Serge
in his letters, in translation
Our liquidation has been prepared
and if they call your name
my hands are tied, my role is limited
to passing through
glass, to letting the glass bend
light around small corners and
translucent wings, *espejitos*
is its Spanish name, but Spain

was lost
      Little mirrors
whose borders are

      opaque
Can I just say one thing
about how everything is lost
one obvious thing about the threat
of sky-glow and the need for dark
oases, and could Serge
be cited, traveling at a constant
speed through opaque objects like
these pages, or would that be
singing, because like ash
when you pass under it
      because like snow
blue systems

NO ART

Tonight I can't remember why
everything is permitted or,
what amounts to the same thing,
forbidden. No art is total, even

theirs, even though it raises
towers or kills from the air,
there's too much piety in despair
as if the silver leaves behind

the glass were politics
and the wind they move in
and the chance of scattered
storms. Those are still

my ways of making and
I know that I can call on you
until you're real enough
to turn from. Maybe I have fallen

behind, am falling, but
I think of myself as having
people, a small people
in a failed state, and love

more avant-garde than shame
or the easy distances.
All my people are with me now
the way the light is.

ACKNOWLEDGEMENTS

Grateful acknowledgement is made to the following publications.

To *Brick*, where 'Index of Themes' first appeared.

To *Aufgabe, The Beloit Poetry Journal, CROWD, The Paris Review, Ploughshares, Post Slope, 26, Verse,* and *Web Conjunctions,* where some of the poems from *The Lichtenberg Figures* first appeared.

To *Beloit Poetry Journal, Boston Review, Chain Colorado Review, Common Knowledge, Conjunctions, Denver Quarterly, Jacket, jubilat, LIT, Passages North, The Poker, Provincetown Arts,* and *Revista de literature hispánica,* where some of the poems from *Angle of Yaw* first appeared.

To *Critical Quarterly* (UK), *Jacket, jubilat, Lana Turner, Narrative, The Nation, New American Writing, The New Review of Literature, The Paris Review, A Public Space,* and *The Seattle Review,* where some of the poems from *Mean Free Path* first appeared.

To *Lana Turner,* where 'The Dark Threw Patches Down Upon Me Also' first appeared.

To *The Paris Review,* where 'Contre-Jour' and 'No Art' first appeared.

I am grateful to Laura Barber and everyone else at Granta for making this volume possible. My thanks to Michael Wiegers and Copper Canyon Press for a decade of support.